NOW YOU ARE MY BROTHER
Missionaries in British Columbia

Margaret Whitehead

Chilcotin children from Anaham on either their First Communion or Confirmation Day, circa 1940s. (BCPM, Ethnology Division, photo no. PN 14000).

Canadian Cataloguing in Publication Data

Whitehead, Margaret Mary, 1937—   Now you are my brother

(Sound heritage series, ISSN 0228-7781; no. 34)

ISBN 0-7718-8275-0

1. Indians of North America — British Columbia — Missions. 2. Missionaries—British Columbia—Biography. I. Provincial Archives of British Columbia. Sound and Moving Image Division. II. Title. III. Series.

E78.B9W54 *1981*   266'.009711   C81-092389-0

47,878

PREFACE

The missionaries of British Columbia have often been viewed with prejudice or jaundice, among other emotions, a phenomenon common to groups whose efforts cause widespread cultural change. This issue of the *Sound Heritage Series* portrays missionary influence on the Indian population by presenting the memories of those who proselytized and those who were converted. *Now You Are My Brother,* as with previous issues, seeks to complement the historical record through oral sources; missionary activity is represented through a wide yet selective range of reminiscences.

The missionaries tell their own stories; there are no doctrines to defend and the morality of watching and participating in the conversion of the native population to a Christian way of life is a quandry readers will have to solve for themselves. There is no argument that, as with any form of contact between cultures with differing values, change occurred. *Now You Are My Brother* speaks of these changes but the author takes no stand on the ethical precepts involved.

The stories cover a broad period of time, from the start of the Anglican missions on the Nass and Skeena Rivers in the 1870s, as exemplified in the life of Robert Tomlinson, to the post-World War Two missionaries of the Cariboo-Chilcotin region, who, like their 19th century counterparts, served a variety of roles beyond their clerical duties within the native communities.

The author, Margaret Whitehead, has been researching and writing about British Columbia ecclesiastical history for several years. In 1981 she published *The Cariboo Mission: A History of the Oblates,* a narrative of St. Joseph's Mission at Williams Lake.

—The Editors

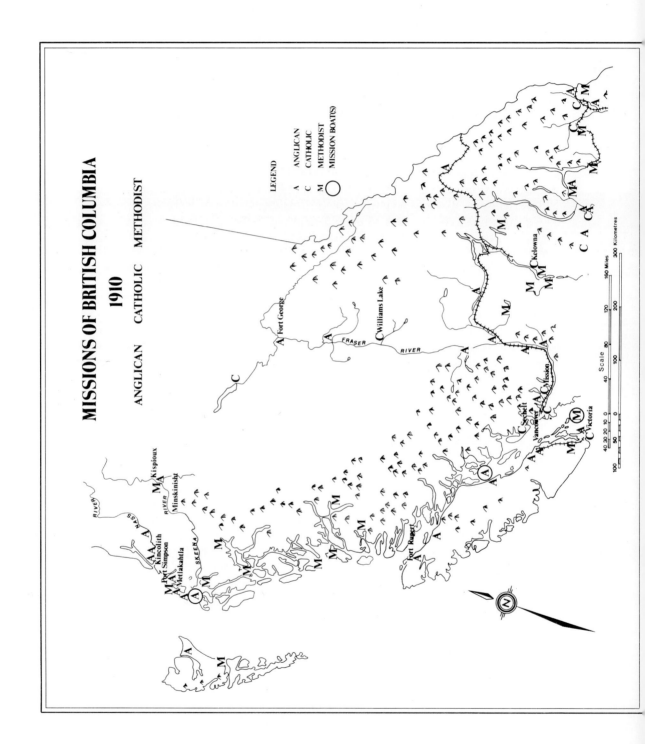

MISSIONS OF BRITISH COLUMBIA
1910

ANGLICAN   CATHOLIC   METHODIST

LEGEND

A   ANGLICAN
C   CATHOLIC
M   METHODIST
◯   MISSION BOATS

Fort George

FRASER   RIVER

Williams Lake

Kelowna

NASS RIVER

Kispioux
Minskinisht

RIVER

Kincolith
Fort Simpson
Metlakahtla

SKEENA

Fort Rupert

Sechelt
Vancouver

Mission

Victoria

Scale

40 30 20 10 0   40   80   120   160 Miles

50   0   100   200   300 Kilometres

N

INTRODUCTION

In 1857, the Oblates of Mary Immaculate (the Oblates) a Catholic missionary order and William Duncan, a lay missionary representing England's Church Missionary Society, arrived to begin permanent missionary work in British Columbia.* Their arrival marked the beginning of a general missionary thrust by the European Churches who sought to "save" the Indian peoples by converting them from "paganism" or "heathenism" to their particular brand of Christianity. The missionaries' methods of conversion were as varied as the religious precepts they offered to their prospective converts, but two methods gained widespread support among both missionaries and Indians; these were the plan for Indian conversion adopted by the Oblate Bishop Paul Durieu and the method of William Duncan.

Bishop Durieu required the Indians to form Christian communities where the rules, enforced by the Indians, were based upon "the commands of God, the precepts of the Church, the laws of the state when in conformity with the laws of the Church, the Indian Act and the by-laws enacted by the local Indian government."† The Indians elected a Church chief, a watchman — who saw that everyone kept the rules — and catechists to teach religion in the absence of the priest. The Oblates were concerned both with the Indians' spiritual and material well-being. Some priests fought for Indian lands and fishing rights and all worked to instill European ideas of hygiene and orderliness. But, under the Durieu System, (as it became known) they were to stress Indian spiritual welfare.

William Duncan was required to follow Church Missionary Society policy and establish communities of Christian Indians which would, in time, form a native Anglican Church administered by the Indian peoples and under the spiritual direction of native ministers. The Indians were to be taught various crafts — for example, canning, carpentry, weaving, and soap making — which would make the young Christian communities financially independent. With this goal in mind, Duncan established in 1862 a community of would-be Christian Indians from the Port Simpson area at Metlakatla, an old Indian village at the mouth of the Skeena River. Within a few years, the community had become a model for others to emulate.

While the Oblates and William Duncan were preaching Christianity and the Indians were appraising the Christian message, another group of missionaries, the first of many such groups, arrived in the Province. The Sisters of St. Ann, a French-Canadian religious order, arrived in Victoria in 1858. As missionary nuns, one of their tasks was the education of Indian children. Over the years, the Churches opened numerous Indian schools; those run by the Catholic Church were most frequently staffed by various orders of missionary nuns.

---

* The first missionaries to British Columbia were the Franciscan friars who came with the Spanish exploration vessels in 1774 and 1775.

† Bishop E. N Bunoz, "Catholic Action and the Durieu System, 1941", History of the Oblates of Mary Immaculate, Microfilm, UBC.

1

In the nineteenth century, missionaries were considered heroes. They chose to abandon the comfort and familiarity of their own cultured society for work within what was considered to be primitive, often barbaric, and definitely pagan civilization. The missionaries claimed as their motives the salvation of sinners and the glory of God. Their mission was clearly understood by the society they left behind and their efforts were recorded in glowing terms by biographers who applauded their work. Today, a more sceptical and secularized society is apt to point out that those biographers were frequently members of the same denomination, if not the same profession, as their subjects. As such, they bolstered the missionaries' heroism at the expense of their more humanizing qualities. Few missionaries have been portrayed "warts and all".

However, those who found their way to frontier territory, whether in answer to a call from God, or the lure of new riches, land or power, were often exceptional people. A close examination of the lives of frontier people often reveals colourful characters leading colourful lives, and the missionaries were no exception. Few people however, including those who would strip the missionaries of their heroic image, would care to live, even for a short period of time, under the difficult and alien conditions — regardless of how colourful they might seem when viewed across the distance of years — which these men and women endured for a lifetime.

Nevertheless, even in their own time, missionaries were not universally loved or welcomed in British Columbia. When towards the mid-nineteenth century the early Catholic and Protestant missionaries made their appearance, the fur-traders regarded them with distinct uneasiness. They were well aware that the sedentary lifestyle the missionaries proposed for the Indians would interfere with fur-trade activities. The traders were dependant upon Indian mobility for the continued success of the trade. In addition, a store opened by the enterprising William Duncan in opposition to the Hudson's Bay Company, caused one trader at Fort Simpson even greater alarm:

> I fear his opposition more than the schooners, in fact if he continues the trade much longer I see no alternative for us but to close up our shop.*

During the colonial period in British Columbia, missionaries were regarded by the governing body as welcome agents of Indian acculturation. Through the truths of the Gospel, the Indians would become as "civilized" as Europeans. Governor James Douglas, for example, encouraged and assisted all missionaries who came to provide "moral and religious training" for the Indians.† In the mid-1850s during the Cayuse and Yakima Indian wars in Oregon and in the mid-1870s during the valiant struggle of Nez Percé Chief Joseph and his people in Idaho and the success of the Sioux against the American army, the government officials of British Columbia needed as many pacifist voices as possible to keep the Indians from imitating their American brothers and turning to war as a means of retaining their land. Often the missionaries did calm the Indians, but some were not above using tense situations to gain advantages for their converts. In 1878, an Oblate missionary wrote to a federal Indian superintendent:

> The Indians in this section are becoming very discontented and using threatening language on account of the delay in settling their reserves. I have used all my endeavours to keep them quiet up to the present but it is evident that they will not heed me much longer in this manner if something is not done for them immediately.‡

* Jean Usher, *William Duncan of Metlakatla*, National Museum of Man Publications in History, No. 5, 1974, p. 67.
† Robin Fisher, *Contact and Conflict*, Vancouver, 1977, pp. 68–69.
‡ James Maria McGuckin to James Lenihan, April 10, 1878, microfilm B-292, C10119, PABC.

The settlers, particularly those farming and ranching in remote areas, also welcomed the missionaries as agents of Indian pacification. For many years, the missionary was often the only white authority figure standing between settlers and unjustly treated Indians. But settlers were far from happy when ministers and priests, interested in the economic as well as spiritual welfare of their converts, taught the Indians the due process of law by which they might appeal unsatisfactory government decisions regarding their land. The Tsimshian at Metlakatla, taught by William Duncan, "were well versed in those mechanics of petitioning and letter-writing which characterize the relations of dissatisfied citizens with their government."*

Some businessmen came to look with disfavour on missionaries, as, like the fur traders, they became subjected to competition from missionary endeavours. In May 1894, R. V. Davison of 150 Mile protested to his MP, F. S. Barnard, that an Indian school established by the Oblates was becoming a threat to his livelihood. He accused the school of using federal financing to manufacture goods "at penitentiary prices" and selling them in direct competition with local businessmen. This was only one of a number of similar accusations made against the school over the next few years.†

The reaction of the Indians to the missionaries appears to have been for the most part quite positive, and by 1904, 90 per cent of the Province's Indian population were nominally Christian. Indians such as the Chilcotin who fiercely resisted all other aspects of white culture accepted Christianity; Indians such as the Kwakiutl of Fort Rupert who successfully resisted Catholic missionaries accepted the Anglican faith. According to the 1939 census, 57 per cent of British Columbia's

---

* Usher, *William Duncan of Metlakatla*, p. 128.
† R. V. Davison to F. S. Barnard, May 21, 1894, RG 10, Vol. 6436, PAC.

William Duncan of Metlakatla (left) and Bishop Paul Durieu, OMI (right). (PABC photo no. 19678 and 76888).

Indians were Roman Catholic, 20 per cent Anglican, 20 per cent United Church and 3 per cent other denominations — mostly Salvation Army. Apparently only 28 Indians were recorded as still holding aboriginal religious beliefs.*

However strong the conversion statistics appeared to be, many Indians retained their old beliefs even while they practised Christianity. The survival of the potlatch which all religious denominations condemned and the continued influence in many areas of the medicine men are witness to this. As one missionary admitted,

> in Africa after anything from five to 10 years, natives have been running their own schools and become bishops. And right here we have . . . achieved nothing comparable. And it has been found that Indians are more tenacious at holding on to their ancestral way of life than any other race we have met.†

As conscientious deliverers of the Christian message, as educators, doctors and sometimes advocates of Indian rights, the missionaries had a profound effect upon Indian adjustment to European culture. It was a tremendous responsibility and many missionaries were living examples of what they preached. But not all. One of the most serious charges that can be laid at the feet of the missionaries is that some led their people into religious controversy. Condemned by missionaries for their centuries of tribal warfare, the Indians had to take sides in not only the centuries-old denominational conflict but also sectarian conflict within established Churches.

There are many instances of the divisions caused by religious conflict and one will suffice as example. In the Skeena and Nass River areas, in which Anglican, Methodist, Salvation Army and non-denominational ministers sought Indian allegiance, there was bitterness between various villages for many years. Mrs. Robert Tomlinson Jr., a former Salvation Army missionary, commented on the situation between the village to which she was sent and the village the Methodist minister attended:

> There was bitterness between the two villages . . . The Indians are clannish and something had happened and they never had services together. But a potlatch would come along and then they'd all amalgamate. But there was that old bitterness. I could go into details but I'm not going to. They were at swords' points with one another.‡

Missionaries have always been controversial in British Columbia and since the advent of Red Power in the United States in the 1960s affected the Indians of the Province, they have been even more prone to attacks. Indians have argued that the missionaries were responsible for destroying much of Indian culture. This is hard to dispute when one reads:

> After his conversion he became very anxious to burn all his idols . . . one Saturday he informed me that it was his intention to destroy them all that night . . . At midnight two boxes were brought in filled with heathen treasures of all kinds, such as the secret whistle which belonged to the man-eater dances, dog whistles, wild dance whistles, aprons, head dresses, leggings etc. these boxes he told me had been handed down for several generations . . . One of the secret whistles belonging to the man-eater dances which he showed to me was in the form of five fingers at one end while at the opposite end was just one piece where the blower was. He told me that the Kitimaat man-eaters had offered his grandfather one slave for this special piece . . . it was to him a great sacrifice. It

---

* Wilson Duff, *The Indian History of British Columbia,* Vol. 1, Anthropology in British Columbia, 1964, p. 87.

† *Williams Lake Tribune,* March 21, 1957.

‡ For this and all other oral sources please refer to A Note on Sources: Biographical Summaries, p. 89.

meant the traditions of his family would be wiped out. At two o'clock in the morning everything had perished in the flames.*

The Indians also claim that the missionaries destroyed their languages by forcing their children to speak only English in school.

Not all Indians, however, subscribe to the idea that the missionaries were destructive. When interviewed, Sechelt Indian Chief Clarence Joe stated:

> Well I think if it hadn't been for the Church, the white man's Church, I think there would have been a total destruction here among the Indians, because they were getting wiped out, you might say, by sickness and by liquor brought in by the white man. The white man was invading their villages and they were taking their women away when they were on their drinking sprees. In my deep thinking, I think the Church was responsible for saving the Indian nation in this country. The more I look at it the more I'm convinced, regardless what Church they are.

However history ultimately judges the pioneer missionaries of British Columbia, it will have to concede that many of them were dedicated men and women of vivid personality, often strong-willed and multi-talented, who succeeded in their task of bringing the Christian message — albeit in a cloak of ethnocentricity — to the Province's native peoples. Their lives added substantially to the richness of the Province's history.

In British Columbia, there were many missionaries — some more influential than others — representing a variety of religious denominations. It is impossible for one single publication to record all their lives and work. The missionaries profiled here were selected on the basis of availability of material. No attempt has been made to present typical missionaries or typical situations. Missionaries, their backgrounds, their personalities, their beliefs, their methods and their biases defy generalization. The views expressed here are the personal views of the speakers.

---

* William Henry Pierce, *Potlatch to Pulpit*, Vancouver, 1933, pp 45–46.

THE "ROMANTIC" MISSIONARY:
Robert Tomlinson

Because of historical interest in William Duncan, other Church Missionary Society missionaries have received scant attention, even though their lives were equally interesting, informative and, in the case of Robert Tomlinson's at least, far more romantic. He followed in the footsteps of his father who was a disinherited eldest son to whom religion meant more than money; he was an impetuous lover who married into Victorian high society; he was a medical intern who provided the only white medical services in hundreds of square miles and he was a staunch evangelical who, in support of his friend, gave up the income from the Church Missionary Society which provided for himself and his family.

As might be expected, the picture of Tomlinson which emerges from interviews with members of his family is one of a man if not of heroic proportions at least of exceptional qualities. Yet, to one of his contemporaries, Bishop George Hills, Tomlinson was a man "full of Irish fanaticism . . . very impetuous and ignorant of the courtesies of civilized society."* It cannot be denied however, that regardless of the bias of his family, Robert Tomlinson's life was always interesting and colourful, and epitomized the romantic aspect of frontier life.

AGNES (KATHY) JOHNSON [Robert Tomlinson's granddaughter]: My grandfather's grandfather was a well-to-do man in Ireland. He was a Catholic, a very strong Catholic. He had a lot of land and property, and money too. My grandfather's father was his oldest son and when he was young he became converted to the Protestant way of religion. His father objected, and he said, "If you turn Protestant you will be disinherited." So he turned Protestant and he became an Anglican rector in Catholic Ireland. When my grandfather was young there were seven boys in the family and of course his father being an Anglican minister in a Catholic country they were pretty hard up.

The mother — my grandfather's mother — had tuberculosis. 'Course they didn't know too much about it in those days. My grandfather said he was going to study medicine so he could learn to find out what caused it and how to cure it. So they said, "We can't afford to send you to college." He said, "If you can't afford to send me to college, I'll get to college some other way."

Robert Tomlinson worked his way through medical training by working initially as a livery boy and later as a tutor to other students. The young Irish boy's interest in tuberculosis resulted in an unexpected diversion from his MD program. When he was still an intern, his father received information from the Church

---

* Usher, William Duncan of Metlakatla, p. 103.

Opposite: Robert Tomlinson, missionary to the Nass and Skeena River areas. (PABC photo no. 41743).

Alice Tomlinson (née Woods), from a carte-de-visite portrait by Federick Dally, circa 1867–68. (PABC photo no. 7366).

Missionary Society that William Duncan needed a doctor as many of the Indians in British Columbia were dying of tuberculosis. Robert Tomlinson looked upon this as a call from God and, leaving his internship incompleted, he sailed for the Pacific Northwest bringing whatever knowledge he had gained to do what he could to help the people.

AGNES (KATHY) JOHNSON: When my grandfather came over from Ireland he had to stop in Victoria to wait for Mr. Duncan to come down and get him. And of course it was in the local paper that he had come to come up north. My grandmother's uncle was the Archbishop [Archdeacon Woods] down there and they invited him to stay at their house. My grandmother was staying there; she was teaching school in a ladies' school for children in Victoria. They got to know each other and they liked each other and she wanted to come with him.

MRS. ROBERT TOMLINSON JR. [Robert Tomlinson's daughter-in-law]: My father-in-law was going off in the north as missionary and he thought it would be a very good thing to have a wife. So he went to Mr. Woods — Richard Woods was his name — and he asks for the hand of his daughter. She was then 16. I guess Grandpa Woods thought he had gone nuts altogether. He said, "Go up there and find out what you're takin' a woman to and if in a year you're of the same mind, you come down and my answer might be quite different. But you're not takin' Alice up there at this stage of the game." So he had to be content with that.

After consulting with Duncan, Robert Tomlinson went to begin his missionary work on the Nass River, where he founded a mission at Kincolith. The following spring, Tomlinson returned to Victoria to marry Alice.

MRS. ROBERT TOMLINSON JR.: In a year he came down with five Indians. You know the Indians had dugout canoes — they were Nishga Indians — but there was not ribs in them. My father-in-law thought in order to bring his wife up he sure was going to have a canoe that was safe from the elements if they got into a storm. So he made ribs and then he made thwarts. Before that the Indians never had thwarts. So he fixed seats in the canoe. The Indians thought that was an awfully good idea, so after that when they fixed their canoes they put seats in. Before that they sort of knelt down and paddled.

Well he was all ready to take her back the next day, because he didn't want these Indians lying around — what would he do with them? Grandfather Woods said, "No. The ladies want to make a wedding and it'll take at least two or three weeks before her dress is made." So he set the Indians to work cutting out a road. The place where they lived was called Garbally, which is "house on a hill" and the road still is called Garbally Road [in Victoria]. They cut that road so that grandfather could bring his bride back to the house in a carriage.

Robert and Alice Tomlinson were married at St. John's Anglican Church and, according to Mrs. Robert Tomlinson Jr., Dean Cridge, a close friend of the family, "walked all the way down to the end of the arm to kiss the bride goodbye." During the nine years the Tomlinsons spent at Kincolith, there were outbreaks of war between the Haidas and the Tsimshians and on several occasions a gun boat was sent from Victoria to the Nass to bring the Tomlinsons out, but they refused to leave. Their confidence that they would not be harmed was based, at least in part, on a strange coincidence.

Two entries from Edward Cridge's 1868 diary. (PABC Add. Ms. 320).

"Garbally," Victoria, home of the Woods family. Drawing by Emily H. Woods. (PABC, pdp no. 1603).

MR. ROBERT TOMLINSON, JR. [Robert Tomlinson's son]: When father was an intern in the hospital in the Old Country he was always losing his laundry when it was sent out to the wash. So he decided to get some indian ink and mark all his laundry with his name. After he got through with that he still had a lot of ink left over, so he thought — going out as a missionary — he might as well have the dove as his crest. And so he made a drawing of a dove on his hankerchiefs and on his linen, and of course being in indian ink that dove was pretty-well black.

When he was in the mission at Kincolith he had two boys staying with him at the mission house. He gave them free room and lodging and in return they were to look after everything, washing included. The boy at the washtub saw the picture of what he thought was a raven, and he came to the conclusion that the missionary came from the same crest as he did.

So he calls to his brother and away the two go down as hard as they could to the other end of the town to tell the relatives that the Shemarget — as they called the missionary — was one of their relatives. He belonged to the same crest, the Raven. There are four crests or clans, somewhat similar to fraternal orders, amongst the Indians.

So they all traipsed back and with their signs and the little English they had learnt, and the little Indian father had learnt, between the lot of 'em he understood they wanted to know, "Was that his crest?" Yes, that was his crest. So they had a feast and it was announced that the Shemarget belonged to the Raven clan, and so the Raven clan had always to look after him. That stood him in good stead many a time later on. Saved his life.

When he brought a bride of course the bride had to belong to some other crest because nobody could marry anybody in their own crest, so she was adopted by the Eagles. And all the children belonged to the mother's crest so therefore when I was born I became an Eagle. That stood me in good stead many and many a time in later years, being an Eagle.

MRS. ROBERT TOMLINSON JR.: When I went up there I couldn't marry an Eagle — he was flying too high for me! So the Finback Whale adopted me. So I was wallowing in the water. Uncle John — I called him — made a potlatch or feast. He adopted me into the Finback Whale crest and gave me two bracelets, which I prize very much.

Although Tomlinson's aim was to develop a second Metlakatla at Kincolith — an aim which was partially fulfilled — his medical training and the lack of any other medical man, forced him into the role of itinerant doctor. This meant that he was away, every year, for several months at a time. He travelled to Metlakatla, throughout the Nass and Skeena River areas, and even, on occasion, as far as Wrangell, Alaska. Alice Tomlinson had to adjust to a very different life as a missionary's wife.

MRS. ROBERT TOMLINSON JR.: She would be alone for months at a time with nothing but the Indian women up there. They were Nishga Indians so Robert, my husband, as a boy learned the Nishga language and could rattle it off before he could talk English because they always had girls in the house working for them, working with them so grandma could teach the girls how to do things. She had never done much sewing herself because they were pretty well protected. They came from Ireland and they belonged to the gentry in Ireland and moved over here. So she'd never done much housework and she'd never knitted in her life. But now she had to teach the Indians how to knit a sock.
    The only way she could learn how to knit a sock was to unravel a sock that was made by machine. The heels are turned entirely different than a home-made sock. So she and my father-in-law figured out how these socks were made and so they taught the Indians how to knit. So the Indians up the Skeena and on the Nass knit their socks with the heels the same way as the boughten socks which comes in from the side. The homemade comes square up. And of course they had to make their own candles; they had to do a lot of things that she had never done in her life.

While Alice Tomlinson was adjusting to a pioneer existence, her husband was gaining Indian trust through his medical skills. His main opposition were the traditional medicine men upon whose traditional role the missionary was intruding. Tomlinson also had to accept that the Indians would not always respond to the services he provided as white patients might.

MRS. KATHY JOHNSON: When he went up the Nass River — one of the first trips he made up the Nass River — he stopped at a village and they brought him a boy that was dying with TB and he told them he could do nothing for him because he was dying. And he explained how the lungs were like bags and that the TB had eaten holes in the lungs and that he wouldn't live very long. When he came back to the village that he had passed through one of the Christian natives came to meet him and told him, "Don't go into the village because if you do they will kill you. They think that you made the sickness because you knew all about it." He said, "I'm going anyway."
    So he went and this fellow told him, "They're going to invite you to a feast and at the feast they're going to kill you." So he went down to the place

11

where they were preparing the feast and they had bearskins hanging around the walls, bearskins to sit on on the floor. And they had kind of a stupid boy — a teenager but rather stupid — tending the fire while they were waiting for everything to cook. So he says to this boy, "What's this?" The boy said, "It's a bear skin." He said, "What's a bear?" So the boy started to tell him all about what a bear was, how it hibernated and what it ate and so on. "Well," he said, "you must have made the bear." "Oh no, I never made the bear." "Well," he said, "how do you know?" "My father told me, my uncle told me, my grandfather told me about the bear." He kept arguing with this boy that he made the bear.

Finally the head men came in and they all backed the boy up that he never made the bear. They *all* knew about the bear. Then he turned round and told them how *his* people had told *him* about the sickness and he wanted to know more and he went to school and he learned more about it. He'd come there to help them but when it got too bad he couldn't do anything. But he was going to try and help them beat the system. And the head chief took a knife out of his blanket and handed it to him by the handle and he said, "I was going to kill you, but now you are my brother."

MRS. ROBERT TOMLINSON JR.: They had a little hospital in Kincolith, the first hospital that was built up north. The Indians brought their own blankets. If an Indian was sick he didn't sleep on any bed. He didn't sleep on any bed anyway, but if he was sick he certainly wasn't going to sleep on a bed and let the bad spirits under the bed. So they brought their own blankets and grandmother administered chloroform — there was no ether in those days — and my father-in-law operated. He operated on a man for appendicitis, just with Alice giving him chloroform. She was the only person who could help at all.

ROBERT TOMLINSON JR.: One time he removed a bullet from an Indian although he was ill himself. He got right out of bed and travelled from Kitwanga up to Hazleton, made the trip in one day. But he was so tired when he got up there — then the Indian was resting easily — so he thought it would be better for all concerned if he waited till he had a little sleep and tackled the job by daylight instead of lamp light. He used one of the old Hudson's Bay clay pipes, brand new one. He sterilized the pipe for a probe. The lead marked the stem of the clay pipe where the bullet was. The bone just scratched it but the lead of the bullet marked it so he could measure it, and then he cut and extracted the bullet out of that. It was lodged in between the bones back of his, oh in his shoulder-blade, in there somewhere.

If anybody called in a medicine man while father was treating an Indian that was the end. He never interfered with the medicine men. If the medicine man interfered with him, well, that's where he stepped out.

It was 46 years father practised medicine and surgery with the Indians — not only of British Columbia but many of the Indians from the Tlingit tribes [in Alaska] used to come over to Kincolith and be treated of bullet wounds and so forth. But for 46 years father treated and he never charged one single Indian for his services. I don't know whether he charged any whites or not; he may have charged some whites but mighty few of them. But that was always considered some record, never to charge an Indian anything for medicine or service.

Opposite: A view of Kincolith photographed by the daughter of Rev. W. H. Collison.
(BCPM, Ethnology Division, photo no. 11428).

He used to buy his medicines and give the medicine free. He was told that the Indian department would supply him medicine. All he had to do was make out an order and send it down to the Indian department and they'd fill the order and send it to him. There was no sense in him paying for the medicine himself when he gave his services. So he tried it when he was at Kincolith. A box of medicines came along all right enough and he opened up the medicine and he looked and he says, "I didn't order that and I didn't order that; I did order so and so." He had a copy of his order and he went down the list.

So he wrote and asked why they didn't fill the order as he had ordered it. Oh, the medicine he had ordered was too expensive. This was a much cheaper medicine; it was plenty good enough for the Indians. He just nailed a lid onto that box and from that day until the day of his death he never ordered another ounce of medicine from the Indian department.

Robert Tomlinson became familiar with many of the native peoples of the Skeena River area and when, in 1878, the Church Missionary Society acquiesced to his suggestion that a mission be started among them, he asked to be allowed to open up the new territory. After a difficult journey over the "grease trail" from Aiyansh — Alice was pregnant and also became ill with typhoid on the journey — and an equally difficult first winter, the Tomlinsons began a new Christian community at Ankatlas. They spent four years at their new mission but it was a turbulant time as the family, drawn through friendship into William Duncan's fued with the Anglican Church, began to feel its effect on their own lives.

In 1874, a schism erupted within the Anglican Church in Victoria. The main opponents were Bishop George Hills and Dean Edward Cridge. Because of his close friendship with Dean Cridge, William Duncan supported Cridge in clashes with the bishop. He also opposed Bishop William Ridley whom the Church

Old church at Kincolith photographed by Rev. W. H. Collison's daughter.
(BCPM Ethnology Division, photo no. 11427).

A view of the Ankatlas mission, 1881. Drawing by Helen Kate Woods. (PABC, pdp no. 1687).

Missionary Society sent out from England in 1879 as the bishop of New Caledonia, an area which included Metlakatla. When Bishop Ridley decided to make Metlakatla his headquarters and began to argue against Duncan's policies regarding the Indians and their development as Christians, Metlakatla divided into two factions: one group, approximately 200 people, supporting the bishop; the second group, approximately 800 people, supporting Duncan.

MRS. ROBERT TOMLINSON JR.: The bishop had a split with Mr. Duncan, and that's a matter of history. Mr. Tomlinson had already started the mission in Ankatlas, which is up above Kispiox. Then there was opposition from the bishop. He wanted them to get out of there and go to Hazleton. Well, Hazleton was a mining town and there was a mixture of Indians and whites. That wasn't my father-in-law's idea of having a mission. His idea was not to mix white people with Indians. So they clashed there. So Mr. Tomlinson went back to England to get orders from the Church Missionary Society. The Church Missionary Society said, "Go ahead with the job that we've given you to do on the Kispiox River."

While in the Old Country he collected money from different churches and he came back and built buildings. He had a small little hospital and improved the mission house and the people came. He had quite a nucleus of people to start this mission. He spent quite a bit of the money. When word came from Bishop Ridley, the letters were in Greek. Alice got the letter and she opened it and here it was in Greek. But when Mr. Tomlinson came home he read it. He interpreted it, "Duncan disconnected." This was written in Greek.

ROBERT TOMLINSON JR.: The Church Missionary Society had sent Bishop Ridley and he, like Mr. Duncan, was a strong-willed Englishman. He was sent out as bishop over the man who had founded the mission. At that time there were about a thousand Indians in the village of Metlakatla. When the bishop came he wanted to use his robes and so forth in church and this was against Mr. Duncan's ideas of what should be. And they wanted the sacraments. Baptism had been observed all along but not communion. He thought they were too close to their old heathen customs where the medicine men were supposed to eat human flesh.

Bishop Ridley, of course, being bishop, couldn't be anybody unless he had his robes on and the experience that father and Mr. Duncan had found out amongst the Indians was that the medicine man was nobody — he was just an ordinary human being — unless he had his medicine man attire on. And if he got his medicine man regalia on then he was superman. So therefore they didn't want the missionary to look as if he was a superman just when he had his robes on in church and an ordinary human being on the rest of the weekdays. But anyway, the bishop insisted and hence the trouble.

Robert Tomlinson sympathized fully with Duncan and expecting more pressure himself decided to leave the Church Missionary Society and, after a brief visit to Metlakatla, go out east and join up with some Moravian missionaries. However, the Indians supporting Duncan asked Tomlinson to remain with them and, in spite of the tensions, the family remained at Metlakatla, eventually travelling in 1887 with the 800 Indians who resettled under Duncan's leadership at New Metlakatla, Annette Island, Alaska.

MRS. ROBERT TOMLINSON JR.: The feeling was pretty hard between the two factions. In fact my husband was out in a canoe one time, and he only had an eight-foot canoe, and first a bullet would go on one side of his canoe and then on the other. The bishop's men were armed. Robert said, "I know that they never intended to hit me, or they could have hit me. But they were sure scaring the tar out of me."
    Another time my husband said an Indian — one of the bishop's men — pointed a gun at him, and a deaf and dumb boy knocked the gun up. Robert said, "I don't think he intended to shoot me then. But the deaf and dumb boy thought he would." I said to my husband, "Why would he do it?" "Well," he said, "I was a cheeky young rascal too. I guess I had my say about the bishop and all his flock and what I thought of them."

ROBERT TOMLINSON, JR.: We lived in Metlakatla — that's Metlakatla, B.C. — we lived there for four years, when the trouble got worse and worse. There was continual fights. Even the bishop himself demonstrated his pugnacious abilities. Right in front of the church he knocked a man down because the man was asking him some impudent question. So the bishop gave him a bump on the nose and bumped him out. And the funny part was that one of Mr. Duncan's elders came up to the bishop and he says to him, "That the way to do the bishop?" And that was his way of expressing himself in what little English he knew, meaning, is that the right way for a bishop to act? Remembering what was written in Paul's epistle to Timothy that the bishop was to be no striker. And here's this fellow sprawled out on the road — on the grass there — in front of the church! Anyway that was the kind of thing that was going on there and went on for four years.

Because of his committment to William Duncan, Robert Tomlinson was left without any means of supporting his family. At Metlakatla, the Tomlinsons were supported by the community and, in return, Tomlinson gave his services as a doctor. However, prior to the Indians' departure for Alaska, another medical missionary, Dr. Bluett Duncan (no relation to William Duncan) arrived to offer his services. Once the Indians had settled at New Metlakatla, Robert Tomlinson decided, in spite of a lack of income, to return to northern British Columbia and establish his own "city set on a hill." *

* Matthew v:14, as cited in Usher, *William Duncan of Metlakatla, p. 152.*

MINSKINISHT: TOMLINSON'S "CITY SET ON A HILL"

The evangelical missionary's vision of creating a native Christian community which would illuminate the heathen darkness surrounding it was based on the premise that the Christian community would be an expression of a native Church. In effect, the white evangelical's role was to be one of guidance until such time as the community, complete with its own native clergy and native lay leadership, could stand alone. By the 1870s and 1880s, the northern coastal regions abounded with newly-created Christian communities, all established by white clergy or lay evangelicals of various denominations; the names Greenville, Aiyansh, Kincolith, and, of course, Metlakatla are witnesses to the popularity of the model society ideal. But how successful were these communities in achieving the ultimate goal of building native Churches? Was the aim of these missionaries to create a viable native Church, or did they lose sight of their evangelical aim and create, instead, dependencies? Did the "city set on a hill" become in fact merely an expression of European paternalism and ethnocentricity?

In 1888, Robert Tomlinson, free of the restraints of the Church Missionary Society — and thus without a form of income — returned to the Skeena River still committed to the ideal of the isolated Christian Indian community. He needed both land and some form of financing and for both he had to depend upon the interest and commitment of the Indian people. It seemed to him therefore a sign from God that he and his family should spend the winter at the village of Kitwanga — where the local missionary offered them his hospitality — in the winter of 1888–89, the winter of a great and destructive measles epidemic.

ROBERT TOMLINSON, JR.: We were at Kitwanga that winter. We were stranded. We were just halfway between everywhere, and that's where we had to spend the winter, at Kitwanga. I was no doctor in those days, but I was good at chopping wood. Night and day we had to keep the fire going. I was the only one that didn't get measles, so the fire had to be kept going night and day. What wood we could spare we gave to those that couldn't get out to get wood for themselves. Father had been working night and day with the sick people from all around. He was just practically worn out.

MRS. ROBERT TOMLINSON, JR.: That was the year of the big measles and Alice busied herself making soup and taking it to the people that were sick. My father-in-law worked early and late with the sick people. The small children that were in their cradles survived the measles, but the youngsters that were running around half-dressed succumbed to it.

It was a busy winter and Robert always felt that it was overruled that they go back there, or else he felt that that village would have been wiped out with

17

Medicine man performing healing ceremony at Kitwanga. Photograph by G. T. Emmons, 1910. (BCPM Ethnology Division, photo no. PN 4192).

the measles. Because grandfather had enough of the know-how to tell the Indians how to take care of themselves, quite a few of them did survive, but there were lots of funerals. And the potlatching went on. Then an old Indian [Chief Hap] gave Robert Tomlinson his hunting ground, which was at Minskinisht. And that was the old name for the place, Minskinisht is "at the foot of the pines" or something — "foot of the mountain."

Minskinisht — or Cedarvale as it later became known — was founded on the Skeena River as a non-denominational mission. Robert Tomlinson had no wish to be attached to any established Church. The basis for Christian teaching was simply the Bible. Minskinisht was never a large village and, unlike most Christian villages, the population was fluid. Some Indians came down from the Nass, others from Kitwanga and Kitwancool; some stayed only for a period of time then returned to their own villages where they acted as lay preachers.

Although it appeared to be a democratic society with decisions made by an Indian council, there was still an element of paternal control. After each family had been assigned a lot, Robert Tomlinson kept the rest of the land for himself, in the words of his granddaughter, "somewhat on the same system that the old squires in the old country used to have, where the tenant farmers worked so long for the head farmer and so on."

ANNIE MOBERLY [Robert Tomlinson's daughter]: I was eight years old. Well, there was nothing here, absolutely nothing! And they just slashed down the trees. There was nothing but trees, wherever you went was trees. And I remember my mother and my eldest sister in the spring used to walk up and down the ice for exercise. And she used to leave me and my youngest sister to keep an eye

18

on the fire because it was a fire in the middle of our cabin. It was an Indian-style house and it wasn't more than about 12 by 12.

AGNES (KATHY) JOHNSON: The Indians used to build their house by selecting trees of about ten inches in diameter and cut them off for posts, the outside ones lower than the middle ones. Then they would take smaller cedar trees and put them across the top of the posts and then use hand-split cedar planking put in lengthways, that is from the eave of the roof to the ridgepole, leaving a space of about two feet in the centre for the smoke to get out. Then they would put a fire all down the centre of the building which served for cooking and heating. In the summertime they had no outside edge on — except maybe a little screening of branches — in the wintertime they hung skins around the outside to keep the wind and snow and so-on out. When the Tomlinsons arrived at Cedarvale — Minskinisht — they did the same thing. They screened off part with blankets so the ladies would have a little privacy, then eight natives slept on the one side of the fire, the eight Tomlinsons slept on the other side.

Then they went and cleaned out all the underbrush, took out the big trees and got enough ground clear to plant their garden for the next winter. They had brought seeds and potato seeds with them. All this garden was planted in between the big stumps. Then they started in and built their cabins and by fall there was a log cabin for each family.

ANNIE MOBERLY: When we started the village father asked them whether they wanted to be down at this end or whether they wanted to be coming this way, you see. "Because," he says, "before we build a church I am going to be the furthest away from the church so that nobody can say they couldn't come to church."

The first money for the new village was raised by trapping furs, and Robert Tomlinson, by-passing the Hudson's Bay Company, collected all the furs and traded them at the coast. For several years the community appears to have been an oddly balanced one. Apart from one Indian couple — Edward Stewart and his wife — who had a little girl, the other six Indians were older couples without families. And, although Robert Tomlinson built a school, for a number of years only the younger Tomlinsons, Indian adults who desired education, and the one Indian girl attended. Mrs. Alice Tomlinson was their first school teacher. Regardless of the small number of people, a governing body was set up in preparation for the time when other families moved in.

AGNES (KATHY) JOHNSON: Then they made a system of how the village was going to be governed, following the Indian system of appointing a council among the chiefs who would control the village, and Mr. Tomlinson acted in an advisory capacity. The community was based on very strict rules. They used the Ten Commandments as the basis for their laws of course, and no smoking, no drinking and very strict Sunday observance. At the time they abandoned all religious or heathen customs. That is one reason there are no totem poles here — although the totem poles actually are historical rather than connected with religion — at the time they all abandoned religious or heathen customs.

ANNIE MOBERLY: Everybody that could, unless they were sick, was supposed to go to church three times on Sunday. Because they didn't know much English and they had nothing to do on Sunday. So there was service at eleven o'clock, there was service at three o'clock — after the service anybody that wanted to stay in

Original church at Minskinisht (Cedarvale) taken June 1906 by Katie O'Neill. (John Veillette, BCPM, Ethnology Division, Veillette no. 73088).

stayed and we could sing a few hymns — then there was service again at seven o'clock in the evening. And then in the middle of the week there was service Wednesday night. It was really to fill their Sunday up because they had nothing to do, and to keep them out of mischief. And they were only too glad.

When the steamboats began to run, father told them they could not load wood. They could not take wood in at Minskinisht and they could not land any freight at Minskinisht on Sundays, just Sundays. So they called it then the Holy City and that's how it got the name of Holy City, from the steamboats, because they thought father was very, very strict.

Gradually, little by little, other people came that wanted to live in a Christian village. Then they decided they'd make a prison. And it was made eight square. It had one window up too high for anybody to climb and it had bars across it and it had a door. There was no smoking, no drinking, no work on Sunday. That was the law of Cedarvale.

There was one man that I know of who was put in jail because he kept running after a girl and he wasn't supposed to. It was against the rule. She was locked up in her house and he was locked up in the prison. Father was the boss but he called in the elders and they'd all decide the thing. They'd all decide whether they should be locked up or whether they shouldn't. They just took him along and locked him in there. And there were books in there, so that anybody that could could read; if they were in jail, they could read.

AGNES (KATHY) JOHNSON: Mr. Duncan believed — and Mr. Tomlinson with him — that the adults should be educated as they were illiterate. They thought the best system would be to teach them to read and write in English, as far as possible. At least to read and write their own names and the names of some places around. Anyone who could say the alphabet and count to 100 was admitted to school — whether they were five years old or fifty years old.

The native language was used entirely for services, during the work periods, and in the home. The Tomlinsons took in any teenage girls that they thought might be a little wild and taught them how to keep house, how to sew and consequently — of course they helped with the work too — the native language was used in the home, except when the family was all by themself or there were white people there — then the English language was used. My dad said that he never heard a swear or a slang word until he was a grown man because the Indians had no slang and they had no swear words, and his parents used good English. My Aunt Alice told me that when she was about 18 she had a severe stomach ache, and she couldn't tell her mother in English because she didn't know the English word for stomach. Indian was predominant. English was a second language — a convenience for them when they went somewhere else.

Although Minskinisht was a relatively small village, it had to have a more viable means of support than fur-trapping. There does not appear to have been the variety of light industry which was found in other Christian communities but there were agricultural pursuits, a saw-mill, canning, and a brick-making operation.

ANNIE MOBERLY: That spring we cleared a little piece of land but it was on the island. Father said that was the best place. We started and we put in some potatoes. Well the next year we increased our place. The Indians made their own gardens but they made theirs way up at "Annawawa" — that's about two and a half miles up further. There's a sort of a flat and they had their gardens there. As soon as we could grow enough potatoes and things, father got in touch with the girls' home at |Fort| Simpson and he'd take down a big two-ton canoe load of potatoes and sell them.

AGNES (KATHY) JOHNSON: They had to have a sawmill because you cannot build lumber houses without a sawmill and there were no commercial sawmills in the country. As Mr. Tomlinson moved from one village to another he started

New church at Minskinisht begun in 1906, completed in 1908. Photographed by Katie O'Neill, February 20, 1908. (John Veillette, BCPM, Ethnology Division, Veillette no. 72018-7).

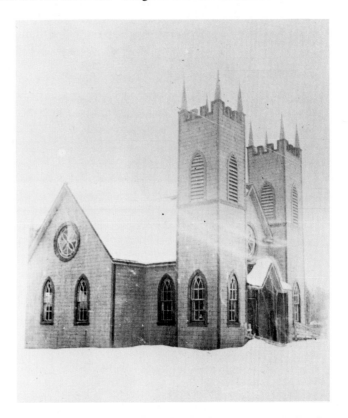

up a small sawmill. Of course these sawmills were paid for by the Church Missionary Society. Mr. Tomlinson had no money. There's quite a controversy over a small sawmill that Mr. Duncan had that he had promised to Mr. Tomlinson for Minskinisht. When the time came, the Church authorities had the building nailed up so that they couldn't take that sawmill out without breaking and entering, which they would not do. Consequently they arrived with no sawmill and no money.

ANNIE MOBERLY: I'll tell you how the sawmill was started. My mother's father and mother died and they left 600 dollars to each of their children, and my mother got 600 dollars. So she said to my daddy: "Here take this 600 dollars and start a sawmill. You can have it." And he started with that. Robert ran the mill with the help of two Indians, Joseph and Philip.

AGNES (KATHY) JOHNSON: All the pulleys were hand-made out of wood. They're really quite a work of art. And the carrier for the lumber was made of wood. They started out with wooden tracks but they found the wooden tracks wouldn't work because when they got damp they swelled and the carrier would go crooked, so they had to put in steel tracks. So they had to buy the belting and the saw and some levers that couldn't be made out of wood, that wouldn't hold. As soon as they were able to get this equipment up the river — that is the metal part — they set it up on Mill Creek across the river. In the meantime, Mr. Tomlinson had taught some of his natives to do very good work with a hand-lathe which he had. One especially was Edward Stewart and he was the one that carved most of the wood for these pulleys.

ANNIE MOBERLY: Nearly all the houses were built — except this one — with lumber from the mill. And you go to Kitwanga, nearly every house that was built at Kitwanga the lumber was bought from here. You go to Skeena Crossing, nearly every house built there the lumber was bought here . . .the old part of the hospital at Hazleton the lumber was bought from here.

AGNES (KATHY) JOHNSON: When they built their houses they wanted to have fireplaces. Grandfather was a great believer in the old-fashioned fireplace. Well, to have fireplaces you must have bricks; to have bricks you must have clay. So they hunted through the woods — when they weren't doing something else — told everyone to look out for clay. Well, "What was clay?" Some of them didn't know. One of the men discovered that there was quite a bunch of blue clay across the river up on the hill. So they went up and they got their blue clay.

They then had to figure out how to make charcoal to cook. You have to cook the clay in charcoal. So he said that they built a kind of a crane out of birch logs and it burned up too fast; then they built one out of cottonwood and it collapsed. Finally they got some green cottonwood and they built a crane that would keep the wood inside to form the charcoal because you have to burn wood with very little oxygen to form the charcoal. Then they made frames — forms — for the bricks. They had the girls working the clay, taking out any imperfections, putting in the right amount of moisture and packing them in these frames. There are some chimneys up the village yet that were made from those home-made bricks.

My grandfather believed strongly in work. One old Indian was telling me — David Wells, he used to live here at one time — he was telling me that when my grandfather was away, my uncle put up some swings just over on the school bank there for the children to play on but when my grandfather came back he said, "There's no time for play, work!" And David Wells said he worked from seven o'clock in the morning till seven o'clock at night with a little time off for lunch, a little time off for supper — but not much — for 25 cents a day, because he was learning to work. The men got 50 cents a day. The same when they worked in the sawmill. They got 50 cents a day and they were paid in scrip.

ANNIE MOBERLY: We had built a little store and Robert Jr. and Richard [Tomlinson] slept over the store. Father said to the Indians, "If I pay you cash" — they wanted him to have a store — "I can't have a store. If I don't pay you cash, I'll write it out on a piece of paper then you go to the store and whatever you get is put on the back of that paper until you finish."

AGNES (KATHY) JOHNSON: The Tomlinson children themselves never attended school outside of Minskinisht. Their mother taught them to read when they were very young, and, as they got older, their father took over their education. But the younger ones, Annie and Nellie, by the time they were growing up their father got occupied with other things and they just got an ordinary schooling. But enough that Mrs. Moberly was able to teach school for a few years here, so it was satisfactory anyway.

ANNIE MOBERLY: We three, mother taught us. And we used to be so glad — or at least I used to — I'd be in school and father'd come in and say, "Oh, I'm so busy, let Annie go and water the animals. Never mind any more schooling." I'd go like a shot. So I had very little. I don't think I got to more than grade five. Later I wrote to Mr. Loring — he was the Indian agent at Hazleton — and I asked him if I could teach the Indian school. And he said, "Yes, if you can tell them what a mountain and river and a stream are, you can teach it." And I taught the Indian school for three years. Do you know what the wages were then? Thirty-three dollars and a half a month. That's all a school teacher got teaching Indians. Of course there were nothing but Indians. No half-breeds, no whites, nothing but Indians.

AGNES (KATHY) JOHNSON: Around about the turn of the century, I can't say which year exactly, the government sent surveyors out here to survey the country and their instructions were that wherever the Indians were resident it was to be made into a reservation. And where there were no Indians the land would be opened up for other people to take up. Wherever a white person was living, they would be given a Crown grant of the acres they were operating or living on, free of charge outside of registration of the papers.

When they arrived here my grandfather said: "I do not believe in sticking them on Indian reserves. If you give the people land that is their own to do with as they wish, they will come ahead quicker. If you put them on reserves you will push them down and you will take away their initiative." "Well," they said, "that's our orders." So they suggested that he take up all the land here himself in his own name so that it won't be turned into an Indian reserve. So he took the whole village on this side of the river in his own name and on the other side of the river my uncle — who was over 21 — took it, and the piece that is now Mountain View Reserve my mother took. So they had the whole thing tied up.

Then my grandfather had a legal lease made out for 99 years for the people in the village for the lots that he had already laid out for them. When he died they found, by trying to straighten the estate, that kind of a lease would

not work in this country. So it was changed, and by that time the government said the Indians could own their land if they wished. So they had it all transferred over to the Indians' names. Then they had to have the government surveyors survey off these separate lots and the price of the survey was divided between 17 and each one was charged just the price of their share of the survey for the lot. And so they have all been property-owning people, paying taxes since that time. And there are very few places where all the natives have been property owners and tax payers for that length of time.

In 1900, a Methodist missionary doctor, Dr. Harold Wrinch, arrived in the Skeena River area. Consequently, when in 1908 the Indians at New Metlakatla sent word to Robert Tomlinson that they needed a doctor, he felt free to go. Richard Tomlinson, the second son, was left in charge at Minskinisht. Robert Tomlinson, his wife, and son Robert, spent four years at New Metlakatla before returning to the Skeena. Shortly after his return, Robert Tomlinson died on September 18, 1913, after having suffered a cerebral hemorrahage.

Minskinisht became Cedarvale in 1913 when the railway came through. Then the post office was build across the river, among cedar trees, and gradually the name Minskinisht was dropped from use.

Minskinisht was the last of its kind. While it never assumed the grandeur of Metlakatla, it did provide a stable centre to which Indians of the Skeena and Nass River country, who wished for a Christian environment, could go. By the turn of the century, however, such communities had become anachronisms. White settlement had spread into what had once been remote areas; mining, large cannery operations, the fishing and lumber industries were attracting the Coastal Indian population, most of whom no longer desired the kind of protection from white culture that missionaries like Robert Tomlinson provided. The era of the "City set on a hill" had passed.

Opposite: First marriage in the new church at Minskinisht, between Agnes Bright and Philip Sutton. Photograph by Katie O'Neill, February 20, 1908. (John Veillette, BCPM, Ethnology Division, Veillette no. 72018-4).

FATHER THOMAS:
A Durieu Disciple

One of Bishop Durieu's most devoted followers was Father François Marie Thomas OMI, a name known to both Indians and whites throughout the Cariboo/Chilcotin country. For over half a century, Father Thomas travelled an immense district, becoming a familiar figure as he ministered to the spiritual needs of Shuswap, Carrier, Chilcotin, Métis and white Catholics. His life was as hard as the lives of the Indians and white pioneers among whom he lived and worked. He had an unquestioning faith and his adherence to Bishop Durieu's methodology remained unaltered in the face of both changes within Indian communities and changes in missionary policy.

Many of the older generations of Indians appeared to have feared as much as respected and loved him. Later generations, accustomed to the religious environment of the Mission school at Williams Lake, viewed him as "just another priest." The white settlers, even in an area where religious bigotry was not unknown, all admired and respected him. Many believed that it was only his presence in the years of white expansion into previously Indian dominated areas, particularly in the Chilcotin country, that prevented outbreaks of violence.

He was respected, feared and loved; he was stern, stubborn and totally reliable. He was unique by being the only Catholic missionary in British Columbia to remain a life-time in one area. Without doubt, regardless of the controversial nature of his work, he is part of the legend, history and spirit of the Cariboo.

In a letter to a fellow Oblate, Father Thomas wrote a "Brief Autobiography" which was to be released only after his death. In a simple and direct way, he revealed his family origins:

> *I was born in the village of Bois de Loup, in the parish of Augan, in the diocese of Vannes, Brittany. I was born of Pierre Marie Thomas, and Anne Marie Menier, both of whom were very religious and wealthy, at 8 a.m. February 19th, 1868. According to the local custom, my father put on his best clothes and went to tell my godfather and godmother of my birth and then all of them, together with the midwife, took me to the Church of Augan where I was baptized on the day of my birth. They had me christened François Marie. I was the 7th child of the family. When I was 6 years old, four of the children died during an epidemic and my father died a year later. I recall little of those days except that, as I was often reminded, I used to climb on to a chair or rock occasionally to preach little sermons.**

---

* François Marie Thomas, "Brief Autobiography", 1950, Oblate Archives, Vancouver, B.C.

Opposite: Father François Marie Thomas. Painting by Mildred Valley Thornton.
(Gaston Carrière, Archives Deschâtalets).

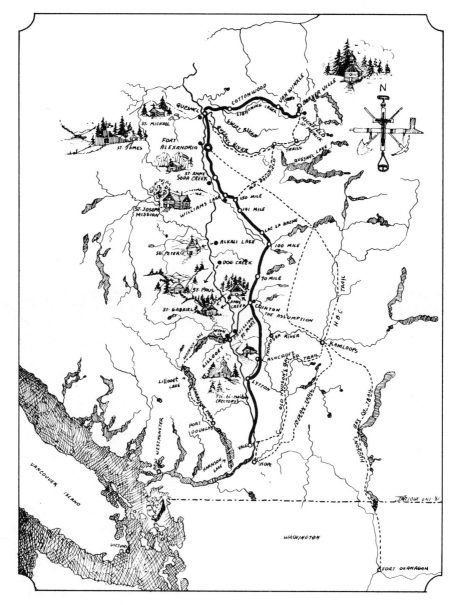

First Roman Catholic churches in the Cariboo. Drawing by John Brioux, OMI. (Courtesy Sono Nis Press).

Perhaps because of the loss of the other children and partly because François was not a strong child, his mother and his uncle, a parish priest, were strongly opposed to the boy becoming a missionary. His uncle insisted that his desire for foreign mission work was "prompted by imagination" and his mother promised him a visit to the Holy Land if he would give up the idea. But François stood firm.

FATHER JOHN HENNESSY: He was not well you know as a child. His mother took him to Lourdes on one occasion. And he wanted to be a missionary and he figured if you were going to be a missionary you had to be a really tough person. So he told me he used to soak nails in water and then drink the rust water. Just to prove he could really rough it!

When he was 18, he joined the Oblates of Mary Immaculate, and in 1894 he was sent to British Columbia as a missionary priest. Upon his arrival at New Westminster he came under the influence of Bishop Paul Durieu, whose system of conversion and Catholicization he came to admire and emulate.

Bishop Durieu took me under his wing as he liked to train his young missionaries himself. After spending 3 months on the missions with Father (later Bishop) Bunoz, I was given charge of the Lillooet, Sliammon, Sechelt and Tloos missions. Between trips to these missions, I was sent to help various priests or taken to North Vancouver and elsewhere by Bishop Durieu who kept on training me for mission work.*

FATHER JOHN HENNESSY: I remember Father Thomas telling me that when he came to North Vancouver he couldn't believe it. He said it was like walking into a monastery. People going in and out of the church all day almost, with the bells ringing. It must have seemed very strange to find devotion like that in such a setting. He had heard so much of the "sauvages" — as the French called them — he just couldn't believe his eyes. So he was trained in that, and he became very, very strict about it.

In 1897, Father Thomas was sent to St. Joseph's Mission, Williams Lake where he was to have complete charge of the Shuswap, Carrier and Chilcotin Indians, and the white settlers of the Cariboo. Although some work had been done in earlier years to gain Indian acceptance of the Durieu System, it was left to Father Thomas to really sell the idea and to keep the Indians faithful to it. It was a task in which for many years he succeeded; but he had to overcome many difficulties, not the least of which was the vast size of the territory he had to cover, and the severe climatic conditions of the Cariboo.

BILL CHRISTIE: He had a territory larger than Scotland, about the same territory I had in the Indian department. He'd have from Clinton, we'll say up to Ashcroft, up to St. Joseph's Mission and then from the Mission he'd go up and then to Barkerville, Wells. That's east of the highway. Then he'd go west. He'd go as far as Ulkatcho, different reserves on the road. There'd be a hundred miles anyhow — more than that — crossing the rivers on horseback. Then from Ulkatcho down to Anahim Lake was another 50 miles. From Anahim Lake to Williams Lake was 200 miles, from Quesnel to Ulkatcho must have been about 200 miles too. And then of course he had Alkali Lake, Dog Creek, Canoe Creek, Gang Ranch and down to Clinton. Tremendous round.

FATHER JOHN HENNESSY: He was the one missionary looking after the whole district. A huge territory. It was unbelievable! He said in the beginning the cold was frightening. He'd never experienced the winters. Coming from France, Brittany, your blood's pretty thin — no matter how warmly bundled up you are.

Several times when I was at Redstone it went down to 70 below. Their thermometer at Redstone measured 70 below. And that's bitter cold. And he'd wake up in the morning with his beard covered in ice where the spittle running down his beard had frozen. And his hands would be blue, so blue that I'd have to do up his cassock for him. I think he was like so many of the older missionaries, they sort of relished doing it the hard way. They seemed to be immune to pain in that way.

It would take a long time for the church to heat up. Very often it wouldn't you know, those old churches were so huge, and everything would freeze. The water and wine would freeze in the chalice. It was *really* cold.

---

* François Marie Thomas, "Memoirs", MS, Oblate Archives, Vancouver.

Our Indians have been trained to take the priest from place to place and cook for him. There are few circumstances when the missionary has to pay from his own money. Most of the travelling expenses are supported by the Indians themselves, sleighs, buggys, wagons, saddle horses and packhorses.

—Father Thomas, "Memoirs".

BILL CHRISTIE: The Indians would take him there, come and get him from the Mission with a team and a wagon. Then he'd go saddle horse to Kluskus and from Kluskus to Ulkatcho, all saddle horse. Then the Anahim Lakes would go to Ulkatcho and bring him down to Anahim Lake, and the Redstones would go to Anahim Lake and take him to Redstone.

DAVID JOHNSON: Yes, when Father Thomas travels amongst the whites he goes on his own little buggy and one horse but when he comes to the reserves we got to go for him. The Alkali Lake Indians used to go for him on the team to the Mission. Stays here for a week. Other ones come and take him from here down to Dog Creek, down to Canoe Creek.

    The reason he made Indians go for the priest: in the olden days one priest got lost goin' on foot by himself to each reserve. It's how the missionary start first time. They were on foot, and one must have got lost. That's why the Indians then were supposed to go for the priest. Wherever the priest is they know it and they go for him on horseback.

FATHER JOHN HENNESSY: He was the one that insisted that they come to him, that they pick him up and bring him to the reserve, feed him, and provide all the food that was necessary. If they didn't do that, he didn't go. They knew that. He would send a letter ahead to the chief, or somebody who could read and write, to let the people know — say at Anaham or Kluskus — that he would be coming at a certain time. Kluskus had to go all the way to Nasko which was 55

Father Thomas outside his cabin on a Shuswap Indian reserve. (Gaston Carrière, Archives Deschâtalets).

miles, and then Nasko people had to go all the way to Quesnel, which was 75 miles. His point was, he said they had to be trained; if they wanted the priest they had to come and get him.

He had most of them trained so that at 4 o'clock in the morning, when it was really bitter cold, the watchman would come in — or someone else — and he would light the fire. Light the fire in the priest's house, then go light the fire in the church. There was another difficult thing, to get wood for the church. So very often when you'd come you'd get the chief to send someone out to bring wood for the church — big logs — and saw them up. And wood for his house, he demanded that. I guess the labourer's worthy of his hire! He never bought a thing. He never bought a piece of bread, nothing, except when we were on the trail. Then it was understood you brought big packsacks.

And this was a word he kept using, *trained*. He came over from the old country with this idea — and it was the picture that was I suppose prominent at the time — that the Indian was a "sauvage." They must be trained like you train an inferior.

Yet he recognized something very wonderful in the hereditary chiefs. He spoke to me of Chief Anaham very, very highly. He said he was a tremendous man. Thomas said, "Royal bearing." He said there was a blue blood amongst the Indians, that there was a royal line. He had great admiration for Anaham and Thomas said there were others like that who seemed to have — as he called it — blue blood in their veins.

A party of Indians from Elgatcho had come 15 miles to meet the Priest. In the following year I paid them a short visit during which I organized the camp according to Bishop Durieu's method, that is to say, I appointed a Chief for church affairs, Captains and other leaders to preside at the prayers said in public, and I appointed a Watchman to attend to the good order of the village. Visiting Indians from Kluskuz and Ootsa Lakes taught them their prayers and I taught the Chief, Captains and Watchmen their duties.
                                                    —Father Thomas, "Memoirs."

LILLY SQUINAHAN: He used to come to the reserves you know maybe once, twice a year, but he'd stay for a week. But he had different rules than Father John [the present missionary]. Drinking, that alcohol, wasn't allowed in his time. If anybody wants to drink, they had to go out of the reserve. It wasn't allowed in the reserve or there was a heavy fine for them. And the dance too. People wasn't allowed to dance.

Our chief at that time, he was a life-time chief. This chief lived 'till he was old and he was a strict chief too like Father Thomas. They had strict rules. In that time when people wanted to go to confession, if they were drinking or if they go to a dance, they had to go first to the chief and tell the chief their troubles. And the chief he'll give them a fine they had to pay before they can go to confession. If any couldn't pay — didn't have money — they'll give something like a cow or even a horse. They had to pay their fine. It went for company money, whatever they give.

BILL CHRISTIE: I was a magistrate. When I first came the Indian agent was a magistrate too. Father Thomas had the thing organized. He had watchmen appointed you see. The watchman would tell him who had misbehaved and he would sit up there with the chief and they'd have court. They'd bring up the

Father Thomas and Indian boys at St. Joseph's Mission, Williams Lake. (Gaston Carrière, Archives Deschâtalets).

prisoners and they got down on their knees in front of the chief and the church. So they'd fine 'em and if they didn't pay, they'd take a horse or cow and sell it and the money went to the church, to buy candles and stuff like that.

The chief could have court himself. And of course the police didn't like this deal at all. But the thing was that the police didn't patrol the reserves. I figured if the chief could handle the situation it was much better. The Indians were quite confused about what was legal and what wasn't, what was morally wrong. If somebody was sleeping with somebody else's wife, they figured that they should go to jail. You see, that's what the Indians couldn't figure out.

FATHER JOHN HENNESSY: When he would arrive at the reserve the first night we'd call assembly of the church and he would tell them his program. He'd set the time for Mass, 6 o'clock or 7 o'clock in the morning 'cause they seemed to get up awfully early. But I found it awfully hard! Then there would be catechism at 10 o'clock for the adults, and for the children in the afternoon. And there would be service in the evening. The next night he would announce that the next day he would hear confessions of only the good people. And the good people were those who had not been drinking or gambling. These were the public sins. Drinking, gambling and eating meat on Friday. I gathered this was the Durieu system.

Sin centred around those three things. Sins against the Sixth Commandment or sins of stealing or lying or cheating or talking about your neighbour, those were not public you see; those were private. They were not considered

Father Thomas with Chilcotin children of Anaham. (BCPM, Ethnology Division, photo no. PN 14010).

great evils. I gather that the reason was those three sins would be disturbing the community. Drinking caused break downs in the family, and quarrels among others. Gambling deprived many of them of the money that they needed, because they were inveterate gamblers. In other words, they threatened the community. Like in the early Church. There were three sins in the early Church; idolatry, adultery and murder. Those were apparently the only sins they had to confess because they all disturbed the young Christian community.

On one or two occasions he appointed a Church chief over the elected chief or hereditary chief, which to me seemed to be undermining this man's authority. The reason was that the hereditary chief or elected chief was not practising his faith, was not giving spiritual leadership or Christian leadership. His thing was to preside over all church meetings, call the people to church, sort of be their spiritual leader.

BILL CHRISTIE: And these Indians were amazin' you know. They'd have church. And the Ulkatchos they hadn't seen a priest for two years; once a year mostly. They'd come in at November first, All Saints, at Christmas, Easter, and they had a church on their own. The chief or somebody would lead the prayers.

I use to spend six or seven days among the Indians giving them a regular mission at each village. Nearly all of them came to the catechism classes held during the day. Another exercise was a review of the sermon during which the Indians were called upon to repeat what the priest had said. There were also practical classes of Moral Theology — something like this: 'John, if someone stole your horse and refused to give it back, what would you do?' 'There would be a fight' — 'And what about the law of God?' There would be a whispered discussion after which John would reply: 'I would notify the Chief, and he would arrange the matter' . . . As can be seen a great deal of trouble was thus prevented.

—Father Thomas, "Memoirs."

DAVID JOHNSON: He preached in the Chinook. He talked Shuswap and he talked Chilcotin. He knows Chilcotin better than Shuswap. There was one Indian named Pete that's the one that is the interpreter for Father Thomas. Father Thomas speaks Chinook and he had an interpreter into Shuswap. Also Father Thomas can speak the Shuswap but he doesn't like to speak it you know; he'd rather speak in Chinook.

CELESTINE JOHNSON: That old woman, Chief Samson's wife, my mother used to say, "She knows all the Chinook. She really knows Chinook. How to read." It must have been easier for them to learn Chinook than learn English. Them old people they never go to school. So Father Thomas must have been a good teacher.

FATHER JOHN HENNESSY: He insisted that I learn Chinook. I can always remember that because one of the first visits we made was to the Indian reserve at Sugar Cane, and I was the first English-speaking missionary that they had met. The rest were all French-speaking. Because there were a number of graduates from the school there and others going to school, they wanted me to preach in English. But Father Thomas wouldn't permit that. He insisted I preach in Chinook and the reason he gave was that amongst the Indians, if you were a man in authority, you always talked through an interpreter. He said that this was the way of the great chiefs. That even if they spoke their own language, they would — speaking to the people — speak through an interpreter. So I learnt Chinook, which was very simple, 132 words.

I was preaching in Chinook through an interpreter. In other words very few of them understood. The old people understood Chinook; more so among the Carriers and Chilcotin than amongst the Shuswap. So the old chiefs, most of them, were the interpreters. Father Thomas had been preaching that way for I don't know how many years.

I soon learned that it was limited in the sense that you could not convey what you wanted to say to them in regard to the teachings of the Faith. The words that we used — religious terms — were all French. Every one of them. There was no Indian word for grace, for sin, or things like that. So there were French words came in like "grâce." What struck me was I don't think the Indians realized what those words meant. The interpreter didn't realize what he was saying, what he interpreted. He would say "la grâce" and carry on you know, mix it up with the Chilcotin or Shuswap language.

I remember on one occasion the Chief, old Charlie Boy at Redstone, was interpreting and I don't know how "la grâce," grace, came in but I was trying to get across some point and he stopped and he said to me, "What the hell does that word 'la grâce' mean?" This is in church, before everybody. And he had been interpreting for Father Thomas since 1897 probably, at least he'd been

Opposite: Father Thomas with Indian postulant (possibly Sister James) at Anaham, circa 1948. (Margaret Whitehead).

34

hearing it. And this was 1935! Almost 40 years. I often wonder just how much we got across to those people you know, in regards to the knowledge of the Faith.

He had this sort of catechetical, I don't know what you'd call it, like a study group. He'd ask them all sorts of questions. One of the questions would be, "Did St. Joseph who was a carpenter ever make a confessional?" That was one of the set questions. It was always the same. There was really no progression in the teaching that was going on, at least that I could see. He would go over the prayers with them, the prayers that they knew like the "Our Father" and the "Hail Mary", that they said in their own language. Just repeating the rudiments as far as I could gather.

When I first went to Anaham in 1897, there were about 275 souls there. A good number of them led excellent lives but the majority indulged in superstitious practices.
—Father Thomas, "Memoirs."

FATHER JOHN HENNESSY: I remember him telling me that this girl in Nasko was sick. She was a Catholic; her father was a pagan. And he sent word to Father Thomas that she was dying, that she wanted a priest. He rode from Quesnel to Nasko, on horseback, 60 miles, all without a stop. Got in and gave her the last rites. But he said before he got there the shaman had been there and there was a smell of sulphur in the room. He believed that the shamans' powers were diabolical. I don't think he ever gave any credit to the fact that they might have been natural healers.

He told me on another occasion, they told him — the Indians — of this shaman who came into the house. He was working on this person, trying to help them, and the stove was red hot and he just put his hand on the stove and nothing happened.

But he was ruthless when it came to them. He would have nothing to do with them. He wouldn't of course allow them near the sacraments, for any reason, until they publically recanted — which very few of them did.

With due ecclesiastical permission, I had to practise medicine but performed no operations. My practising medicine helped fifty per cent in surpressing the witch doctors and did a great deal more than that.
—Father Thomas, "Memoirs."

FATHER JOHN HENNESSY: Father Thomas had made a study of medicine before he came, for about a year — particularly the use of herbs and roots. More or less in the use of the natural medicines. And he carried quite a supply of what you'd call native medicines.

SISTER PATRICIA: He was a doctor as well as a priest. He made all kinds of medicine for the Indians. And some of it was very good you know. When he'd be in from the missions [at St. Joseph's] he'd be in the kitchen cooking this and that. The bark from this tree is good for that. Herbs that are from such a place are good for that. He had all kinds of bottles. I didn't use any but he used to give the Indians medicine. They had a great faith in it too.

FATHER JOHN HENNESSY: He had all sorts of grease, bear grease, coyote grease, and he maintained that they were very volatile. They'd be absorbed by the body say, much quicker than the ordinary linament you might use. He maintained the bear grease was excellent for the hair if you put it on; he was bald when he told me this so I guess he never tried it! He smelled to high heaven! He had snake oil; he would catch a snake and boil it and then skim the oil off. He maintained it was very good for the eyes. He used to bring lots of licorice; maintained this was good for their health.

He would get them to bring bear grease, and another was the grease of the beaver. And he had this in jars and he would give it to them if they had aches or pains, to rub in. Also he had brandy and he would put in the brandy something like peppermint that would colour it and take the taste away and if someone was really ill and he figured they needed a shot of brandy, he would give them that. He was the only doctor around; there was not another for years.

I noticed that they became less wild and that, as the years went by, their mentality improved even as regards superstitious practices. . . . An Indian doctor promised me to give up his practice and signed a paper with his cross. Three months later, when I was at Canim Lake, at a distance of 140 miles, he returned to his practice so as to cure a child. Twelve days later the Indian doctor and the child died.
—Father Thomas, "Memoirs."

FATHER JOHN HENNESSY: They were very nice with him and he'd joke with them but I noticed that when he was meeting them he'd be very stern. And if the person was living in sin — quote, unquote — not married, he wouldn't shake hands with them. And I gather this was supposed to be part of the Durieu System — that you did not communicate with those who were not living according to the way the Church wanted them to live as Christians and Catholics.

They feared him. More than once they would say to me, "You see that man over there?" — he'd be shaking with the palsy — "Father Thomas put the eye on him." Something to that extent. He had looked at them and this had caused this sickness. They were afraid if somehow he was involved, that he could put the evil eye.

LILY SQUINNAHAN: He used to travel by wagon that Father Thomas and many times he had a runaway but he *never got hurt*. And the driver does, but *he* never got hurt.

FATHER JOHN HENNESSY: This man was an Indian doctor and was dying. They called for Thomas and he refused to give him the sacraments until the man recanted. Of course when you're dying you'll do anything. So Thomas wrote out a paper on which he recanted of his being a shaman and promised never to practise again. And the fellow signed it — with just his mark — anyhow he signed it and Thomas said, "Here, you keep one" — there were two copies — "I'll put the other in the church." And he put it in the empty tabernacle.

The old man got better and of course feeling hale and hearty he began practising again. And didn't he drop dead of a heart attack! His wife went to the police and accused . . . charged Father Thomas with the murder of her husband, because of that paper. The police said, "Well, where was Father Thomas?" And he was 150 miles away when the man died. She said it was that paper, that paper in the church had killed him.

When he went to Marguarite or Alexandria — the reserve was Marguarite — there was a trial on and he was called in. It was a public confession, a culp. This lad was adamant. He was accused of having done something and he denied he'd ever done it. Thomas came in and he put his glasses on. They

Father Thomas resting in front of St. Joseph's Mission, Williams Lake. (Gaston Carrière, Archives Deschâtalets).

interrogated the Indian again and he confessed to the whole thing. They said to the Indian, "Why did you suddenly decide to tell us, to confess?" He said, "Long ago my father told me that the missionary was here and he said that, 'You people lie, but one day there's going to be a man come here with four eyes and he'll know your inner thoughts.' I saw that priest Thomas and the glasses." He told me that himself, so it obviously happened.

Sometimes they hid some public misdemeanour such as a pagan feast or drinking party. However, the white people informed me of many things, including drinking parties and superstitious practices which the Indians hid from me. The Indians behaved well during the missions in spite of the horse races held on the reserve, a recreation which Bishop Durieu permitted provided that they were held outside hours set aside for religious exercises. I believe that I can say that, expecially insofar as drinking is concerned, that 1914 to 1939 was the Golden Age at Anaham and in the other Chilcotin reserves. Most of these people would go through fire to receive Holy Communion. Why? Because to receive Holy Communion they had to give up their public faults.
—Father Thomas "Memoirs."

Unfortunately Father Thomas' "Golden Age" came to an end, although in spite of evidence to the contrary, he never gave up his faith in the devotion of the

38

Indians. He demanded of them what he would not demand of white Catholics, namely that when they came together for a religious celebration, they continue the way of Bishop Durieu, and that they abstain from drink. It was a demand that might have been realistic in the late eighteen and early nineteen hundreds, but it was totally unrealistic in later years. The Indian peoples of the Cariboo had accepted the Durieu System in earlier years; now the younger generations rejected it.

BILL CHRISTIE: Most of these reserves were just occupied during "priest-time" they called it. Of course once the missionary left they usually got making home-brew and have a bit of a celebration. You couldn't blame them for that.

FATHER JOHN HENNESSY: If the mission lasted on for a full seven days [the drinking] would start. I think through sheer boredom. What are you going to do all night? There was no television. They had a radio that brought in a little music. From seven o'clock on it was pitch-black, dark in the winter. Some would start drinking and then others would get caught up in the crowd you might say. In the summer it wasn't bad because they'd have races. They were good at that. They'd have great horse races, foot races.

In spite of evident changes in Indian life-style created both by the effects of increased Indian/white contact and more formal Indian education, Father Thomas stubbornly adhered to a missionary program which even in earlier days had not gone uncriticized and which later generations of Oblate missionaries were finding totally unacceptable. It was not until Father Thomas' retirement from active missionary work in the early 1950s — after an unprecedented 55 years in one area — that the Durieu System finally passed out of existence in British Columbia.

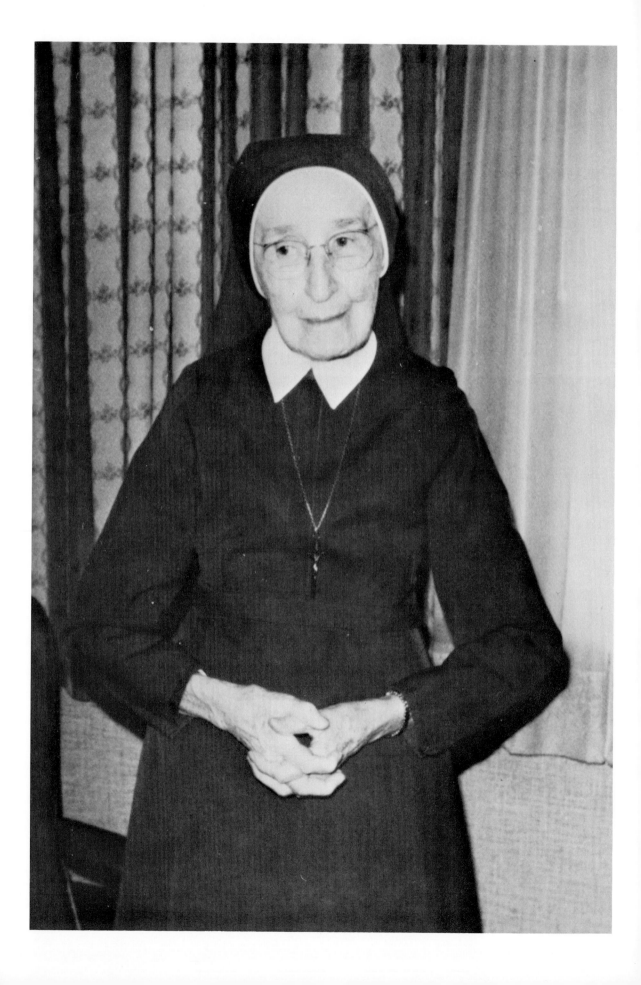

A MISSIONARY SISTER REMEMBERS

Sister Patricia, christened Josephine Tuite, was born in County Meith, Ireland, in 1893. Her father was a farmer and she had four sisters and one brother, none of whom entered a religious life. Initially she went to a national school run by the English government and her teachers, though Catholic, were not nuns. From the time she was eight or nine years old, the young Irish girl felt that she would be a nun. She had cousins who were nuns and whom she visited several times but they were not in a missionary order and Sister Patricia "liked better to go on the missions, to go among coloured people. Preferably to Africa." In preparation for joining a religious community — although she had not yet decided which — at the age of sixteen she attended the missionary school run by the Sisters of Mercy at Callan. In 1911, Mother Aimée de Marie, regional Superior of a French order, the Sisters of the Child Jesus, that had begun missionary work in British Columbia in 1896, visited the missionary school. Bishop O'Neil of Vancouver had given Mother Aimée the address of the school and she had come to recruit young women for the Indian missions in British Columbia.

The Sisters of the Child Jesus had entered British Columbia at the request of Bishop Paul Durieu. Catholic institutions, including residential schools for Indian children, were developing rapidly and the Bishop needed help. The first four Sisters arrived in 1896 and were sent to the newly-opened residential school at Williams Lake. In 1898, several other French sisters arrived and three were sent to St. Paul's School in North Vancouver to teach Squamish Indians. Two years later five more arrived and were dispatched to work at white schools in New Westminster. In the fall of 1910, 10 Sisters, fleeing the French government program to secularize their order, came to Canada and several taught at an Indian residential school at Squamish. In 1909, the community opened St. Edmund's Catholic School in North Vancouver and the following year the Sisters accepted teaching jobs at Our Lady of Lourdes parish school in Maillardville, the home of numerous French-Canadian families.

Although she had desired to go to Africa, the young Irish girl was so favourably impressed by Mother Aimée that she decided to join the French order. Six months later, in the company of Mother Aimée and two French girls, she left for Vancouver, a place of which she had no knowledge but which sounded to her "very far away." None of the young postulants who joined the order and travelled to Africa, Australia, New Zealand, the United States and Canada knew very much of

Opposite: Sister Patricia, Sister of the Child Jesus. Photograph by Margaret Whitehead, June 1979. (Margaret Whitehead).

the indigenous peoples they were going to serve. All that Sister Patricia knew of the North American Indians was that in Ireland they were known as Red Indians. In 1911, Sister Patricia journeyed across Canada to Sechelt, where she and her companions were welcomed as the first postulants to the newly-opened novitiate. Sister Patricia was the first English-speaking representative of her order to British Columbia. Another first was the arrival of an Indian girl, a Shuswap from Williams Lake, whom Bishop Durieu hoped would be the first of many native religious vocations.

SISTER PATRICIA: I made my novitiate at Sechelt. There was an Indian school there at the time and our Sisters were in that school. I'd never seen Indians before. I did find their skin was different but they seemed to be very amiable, very gracious. I thought they would not be civilized. In fact I find they were more then, than now. When you offer yourself to come on the missions, you're not worrying about what you're going to meet. It's understood that you would just get along and there'd be no point even to think of going back.

     Our novice mistress was there also. She was Mother Thérésine; she was French. There were two postulants who came out from France and there was an Indian girl from Deep Creek who had been at school at Williams Lake, at the mission. Later on she was transferred to Prince Albert, Saskatchewan. We had Sisters there. This was in 1918 because she died of the flu in 1918. She took pnuemonia, Sister Henrietta didn't pull through. The Indians were not very strong, she was not able to fight it. She was one that didn't speak much. I never heard her criticizing anything but she had a very hot temper. She struggled . . . she got over it. She'd just pick herself up and that was all. She wouldn't even say anything. She had a lot of will-power, 'cause it must have been a terrific change for *her*, although she had been at school up there for at least nine years. She knew the Sisters very well. There was good discipline in the school at that time. She was something older than I was, I'd say she was about eighteen or nineteen. Others came later on. They stayed, some of them quite a few years, but finally left.

    In 1957, Father Thomas wrote of Sister Henrietta: "A Shuswap, prepared by Father Boening then principal of the Cariboo Indian School, entered the Novitiate of the Sisters of the Child Jesus and died at their convent in North Battleford when she was about 26. She was perhaps not as happy (in religious life) as a white girl might have been."*

SISTER PATRICIA: The Indian children were there at the school. I found everybody very nice and kind and friendly. I didn't get homesick or anything like that. Sechelt was a very quiet place. In those days, oh, it was a beautiful place. In fact there was just the reserve and the school and a store which was the post office at the same time, and a hotel. That's all. There was the Indian reserve right on the shore. The brick school building was up on a hill, not a very high hill but a good elevation. They had orchards around the school, they'd flowers, a nice lawn and fruit, lots of fruit, and orchards boys' and girls' sides. There's a big expanse of open sea there. You could see Vancouver Island and that's gorgeous you know. It's just lovely. Those who like swimming could swim every day, in summer anyhow. The children would swim I don't know how many times a day in summer. We were very much to ourselves. Nobody bothered us.

---

* Letter of Father Thomas to Father George Forbes, nd, Oblate Archives, Vancouver, B.C.

Knitting and sewing lesson given by the Sisters of the Child Jesus, St. Joseph's Mission, Williams Lake, circa 1900. (PAC, National Photography Collection, photo no. C-56765).

When the Sisters arrived at Sechelt in 1904, Mother Aimée had been less favourably impressed. She commented, "In spite of the charm of the place, I was oppressed by the thought that on the morrow when we would return to Vancouver, our Sisters would remain here, that they would struggle far from us, alone against problems, anxieties and the privations which accompany a new foundation." Mother Thérésine, the Sechelt superior, later wrote, "We immediately went to the chapel where there were as yet neither chairs nor pews. As substitute we used a plank upheld at each end by a crate. It sometimes happened that the convent kitchen was deluged with an awesome quantity of game, while at other times, scarcity was the order of the day, week, or even month.*

SISTER PATRICIA: We got to know the children and the Indians down the reserve. They were very friendly. They would come up to see the children. The children got home sometimes for weekends. You got to know all the Indians, little by little, like that. And they were really good. They practised their religion very well. They'd wonderful faith. Those Indians who couldn't write or couldn't read, they could sing the whole Mass in Latin. The whole thing. The Kyrie, the Gloria, the Credo, the Sanctus, the Agnus Dei, the whole thing in Latin. When there was Mass for the dead — which was a difficult air — they could sing that whole thing. There was an Indian man, a Chief Gaspard — later on the whole family went over to the name of John — and that man could fill the church on his own. He'd a powerful voice. Those Indians could sing every hymn nearly in the book. It was quite hard because they hadn't been at school. They knew their religion. We often marvel at that. Now children complain if they've two lines, if they have that much to learn by heart. That

* P. Coran, S.J., *Messengers of the Holy City*, Lyon, France, 1969, p. 150.

was the most wonderful thing that I found. And it was the same on all the reserves. Different language but they knew everything by heart. They went to church. They had a beautiful band . . . Christmas, midnight Mass, they had the band inside. It was the missionaries taught them all that they knew.

CHIEF CLARENCE JOE: People are wondering how come we don't take part in Indian potlatches as you see in several reserves. . . . The Sechelt was so attached to the Church they did away with their own beliefs, own Indian songs and dancing. They set their minds to one thing, their church. As early as 1868. I wouldn't say the church forced them.

SISTER PATRICIA: We the postulants used to supervise study periods and there were some backward children we'd give some remedial help to; we were not among the teachers. The children boarded. You see the parents would go out fishing or logging or be away for months at a time. So it would be impossible that the children would be with them. The school was built by the Indians not the government. Well, they did all the work. Where they got the material I wouldn't know.

CHIEF CLARENCE JOE: In 1945, the government asked us if we would turn over our boarding school to the government and they in turn would build a day school for us. At that time, a few of the old chiefs still lived — they said no, the school belonged to us.

SISTER PATRICIA: At that time the children were very obedient. They worked quietly in school. They were very polite. They were easy to manage in school but you know they were not too reliable — although they didn't run away much at Sechelt. Anyhow they were close; where would they go?

The girls did all kinds of fancy work and sewing. They were very industrious. They liked to work. And this was what they needed after school life, how to make clothes and how to mend. So the seven Sisters were busy with them. They had children on their hands all the time. Night and day. When lay people took over, they were maybe three times seven.

When I left the novitiate I went to Maillardville, a French-Canadian town about three miles from New Westminster. It's called after Father Maillard. He had a lot to do with founding that place really. I stayed there a year. I was teaching an English class there. That was what I'd call my first obedience after leaving the novitiate. I would like much better to be on the missions. Then the following year I went to Williams Lake. I travelled with two other Sisters. We went by train to Ashcroft and then we got a car. Cars were very scarce in the Cariboo. They had no car at the mission and we took certainly a couple of days to get to the mission from Ashcroft. It was a gentleman who lived not too far from the mission. He may have been the only one who had a car around there at all. I thought we'd never get there, there were pine trees and all rocks.

St. Joseph's Mission was a very neat-looking place. It looked like a little village. Several buildings you know. They were white, had galvanized iron roofs, and it was a very attractive looking place. Beautiful countryside around. The boys had their classrooms in their building and the girls had theirs in their building. The convent was in the same building as the girls. It was a long building about three storeys. Of course there were mosquitos. They were new. And then in winter it was very cold. Oh, fiercely cold. There were a couple of furnaces. We had to get wood into the basement. The boys and

Oblate Brothers would cut it, saw logs about three feet and then they'd split them. They were heavy pieces to get into the furnace. And it took an amount of wood when the weather was really cold, and yet you couldn't say that the house was warm. It was very cold.

Everything was very primitive. I mean we did not have the conveniences of today. There was running water but just cold water. You had to heat water in boilers if you wanted hot water. Wash days were quite a thing you know, the tub and the washboard. We didn't have a plentiful supply of water, we had to keep the same water.

All the Sisters who were there during my first eight years they're all dead now. There was Sister Gabrial and Sister Fabian — she was there over 20 years — and Sister Assumption and Sister Seraphim and Sister Stanislaus; she was Irish. There was only Sister Fabian of the four who opened the school.

The children were hard to understand. They seemed to mix up all their letters, all their consonants especially. For "b" they would pronounce "p" and everything was mixed up. Now for instance, for "sheep" they would say "seep" and then for "see" they would say "she". They'd use "she it". And it was odd. When they wrote they put the wrong letters you see. They put "It's very gold in the morning". I don't really know why the children did that. And they kept it, more or less, a long time. Nowadays it's better, but it was a problem at that time.

The children were mainly Shuswap from the reserves around. There were maybe six Chilcotin in all. They were very intelligent, the Chilcotin. It was a

St. Joseph's Mission, Williams Lake. (John Brioux, OMI).

Missionary Sisters of the Child Jesus with Shuswap and Carrier Indian girls at St. Joseph's Mission. Interviewee Celestine Johnson is on the far left, front row. (Celestine Johnson).

long distance for them to come and I don't think they were ready for school at that time. They're a different type of people altogether than the Shuswap. They like better to keep on their own. They didn't want to mix up with others. The children were the same. They had their own group and that was it. They had to go along with the others but they didn't speak the same language either.

There would be a hundred, I mean the two sides, the boys and the girls. That's all the accommodation that was at the mission then. We were two nuns on the boys' side and there were two on the girls'. We always taught the same classes. There was one Brother disciplinarian on the boys' side. He had charge of the boys out of school. They did manual work. He supervised that and he was with them at night in the dormitory and the dining room. Every place. I was on the boys' side with Sister Seraphim. The boys were easier to handle than the girls. They always had difficulty with the girls while we didn't with the boys. The boys were far more obedient and they were easy to please. A very small thing would make them happy, a little gift or anything, while the girls were more capricious and very, very hard to please.

They were not mixed but later on they did mix them. At least the intermediary were mixed, in later years. But they had changed somehow. They opened up more. You see the Indians were very hidden, and except they had a great faith in somebody, they won't tell them anything. Closed. Oh yes. Very closed off. I suppose they're shy and they're very greatly afraid to make mistakes. It's strange. And they notice every little mistake that their companions would make, or that anybody would make in fact. They were keen that way. They observed everything.

We were under the government and we had to follow the white school as far as possible. The children were slower, but we took everything the white schools had. We had grade eight. And there were some very intelligent children. They used to do the papers that the grade eight got for their entrance exam. Before going into high school, grade eight had to pass an exam, which was quite difficult. I'm sure it was as difficult as they had given grade ten today. If they passed this they were ready for high school. So some of them passed. They were not going to high school, they had no high school then. But at least you could see they were doing just as well as the white schools. To grasp everything in English and be able to work on it after, get an exercise to do, well they had to pay attention. We used to have very good grammers. There were lots of exercises in that you had to do after you got the lesson. There were blanks that you had to fill in and put the right word in the right place. This was hard, if you were not attentive, expecially for the Indians. English was not their language and they had to be sure. They had to listen. They were good writers, their handwriting, their books were neat. There was no printing in those days. You started writing in grade one.

There was a lesson on General Washington. How General Washington was always punctual. To speak about the States, even to speak about *Vancouver*, they just couldn't figure it out. They'd never seen an automobile. They got their first car at the mission in 1917, I was there. That was a marvel for the children. They had their Indian reserves, and 100 Mile House was the place where there was a post office, there was a bank, there was a hotel and store. 150 Mile House, that was there, but Williams Lake, *nothing*. Just the lake and the school. That's all there was. The white children up there had no more.

Sixteen was the age the Indian children left school. But some stayed longer because they wanted to stay on. I guess they liked the mission and they knew that going home life would be much harder than it was at school. Their first high school was at Kamloops but that's years later than then. But you know, in one sense I think it was better for them because they learned what they needed at home. They learned housekeeping, they learned cooking, they learned baking, they learned making and mending clothes, and this is what they needed. Now they learn a lot of things, but they won't keep a job. So we find that they lost that way. They got away from their Indian culture.

CELESTINE JOHNSON: When I think about it I think that school at the mission was strict. But now I say it was good. We had to learn everything, sewing, cooking, everything. Now in these days at school they don't know nothing — no sewing, nothing.

SISTER PATRICIA: And the white people around were always glad to hire an Indian girl during the holidays because they said they're clean, they know how to work and they give satisfaction. They would never be looking for jobs if they wanted to go to work. They learned housework, how to keep a house clean. Everything. The boys had manual training. They had a special man there that taught them all kinds of woodwork. Some of them made beautiful furniture, you wouldn't believe that it was made by an Indian boy! They were very skilled. And of course they helped with the farm work in the fall when they were bringing in the crops.

You see school was from eight-thirty in the morning 'till noon. Then, in the afternoon, they didn't go back to school until four o'clock. So the boys worked outside like that.

They were good workers. And the girls worked in the sewing room. They had mending to do and making. They made most of the clothes that they wore, at least the underclothes like shirts and everything. Those were all made at the

Missionary priest and school principal Father Rohr (centre), Sisters of the Child Jesus, and Indian girls at St. Joseph's Mission, enjoy a sunny day and gramophone music. (John Brioux, OMI).

mission. There used to be, oh they called it a fair or sort of exposition at Williams Lake and they would put fancy-work there and some school work, copy books and their penmanship. Oh they were getting prizes! It was excellent work. And their art, their needlework was far better than the whites could do. They were artistic in their own way.

After the mid-day, lunch, everybody had something to do. There was a lot of dishwashing. There were girls named for the boys' dishes and there were a lot of them. Then for the priests' dining room, there was somebody else. There were the men who worked on the mission farm — and there was always a good number of them — they had their dining room. Then there was the kitchen and the girls' dining room on the other side. And the Sisters. So there was a lot of dishwashing at noon. And then those who were not on dishes were bringing in wood. We'd go to the woodpile and load them, give each one a piece; she'd go and throw in down . . . there was a slip going to the basement. There were no idle moments.

We had recreation then at evening, after supper. Well you know these children could play with anything. They'd get in a ring and they'd sing. They had all kinds of games of their own invention mostly. But they could play with anything. And then there were certain seasons of the year, if you followed that it was very interesting. Like in the spring now, when the bushes and shrubs began to grow and get leaves, then they would cut branches or sticks from that and they'd make whistles. Everybody! I don't know where they got the knives but everybody seemed to be able to make a whistle. And then another season was making rag balls, pieces left over of what we cut out of something that they were going to mend. And it was rag balls. Everybody seemed to be able to make a ball, and they'd throw it over the lower roofs. Oh but they were hard to touch. They were well-made. Another time they'd have oh, the mud season. It was terrific. You know the mud up there is like glue. So mud pies. They'd go up the top of the yard where there was a little elevation and everybody would be sitting down and not a word! They'd be too busy making mud pies and

48

getting into a mess. So all these seasons passed every year. You could get ready; you could follow. The boys it was marbles, or thing like that. They had their play too.

We never remarked anything different from other children really. They could easily get a good time out of very little. Imagination! In spring and summer their recesses were outside and they had swings and they played baseball. At least all the bigger boys played baseball. The little ones would swing or make houses. Tents. Wigwams. Every kind of stuff. And it went up fast you know. You'd wonder how everybody could find material to do this. That was the wonder. Another time it would be string, a piece of twine. Everybody seemed to have twine but where it had come from? They'd make it with their fingers and they'd say, "Sister, look that's a fence and that's a house." All kinds of imagination.

And they had very nice voices. They were wonderful singers. They used to be taught songs. Hymns and songs too. They could sing well. In those days we had the organ. All the church music was organ. And there was a piano too, but it was the organ they used for singing. They learned a lot of nice songs too. You know World War One and World War Two were on while I was up there and there were many nice songs that were composed then, during those wars. So they learned all those and then "The Maple Leaf" and all the Canadian songs. No Indian songs. Well, they'd sing hymns. Not the children but those who were grown up — their parents — they'd sing Indian hymns. The first missionaries taught them hymns in Indian but they used the French melody. You could follow the air, it was very good, but you couldn't get the words.

It's a very difficult language. It's all gutteral. Seems to be lots of "K's" and "W's". Shuswap is a very difficult language. Here and there I learnt a word. The Carrier language is much easier. There was a lot of French in the Carrier language.

The Indian parents could come to visit when they wanted to. There was a special room we called the Indian parlour that was their room. Usually on Sundays they were coming but some would come and put up their tents some place around and stay several days. Oh, they had all liberty that way. The children couldn't go during school or that, but at free time they could go. Alkali Lake was 40 miles away and Canim Lake was about 80. Chilcotin was much further. They had only buggies and horses in those days. So it took them a few days to get to the mission. And their way is not hurrying you know. They don't hurry. Even if it's pouring rain they walk very slowly. Don't mind getting wet! It's a happy disposition.

The children were very happy. Some didn't even want to go home during the holidays. They preferred to stay at the school. If they had parents, or a home it was better that they go. We had to make our retreat during that time and we were six, so three would come down to Vancouver; the others would stay. When the first three came back the others went. There was always Sisters at the mission. There was plenty of work to do during the holidays. There was still the cooking for the men, and for the priests. There was house cleaning and washing and canning vegetables. There was a big garden. They'd bring the vegetables not in pails, in those zinc wash tubs, well, *that* full of peas or beans or rhubarb.

The children certainly did lose during the holiday because it seemed they had to begin all over again. They were kind of silent. They were chewing gum. Well the gum, they used to get it in the trees. It wasn't bought, the real good stuff I suppose. They were not so friendly for a while. They wouldn't talk like they did before. They seemed to be — in their mind — some place else for a while. Then we'd a lot of cleaning up to do.

You see when they were at school they wore the school clothes, as we called them. They were supplied with everything. They'd plenty of clothes, good clothes, but they were all government clothes, or school clothes. And then they washed their own clothes that they brought back and they were put in their suitcases and brought to their lockers upstairs. They didn't use them again until they were going home again. So they were always dressed in school clothes. They didn't bring the school clothes home, or they didn't use their home clothes in school.

When talking about her school days at the mission, Celestine Johnson of Alkali Lake recalled, "We weren't even allowed to talk Shuswap at the mission. Sisters won't even let us. If they hear us talk they punish us. Maybe they were scared we'd talk about them! We talked Shuswap when we were alone." Her husband David added, "But them French teachers you know they don't really pronounce their sounds right. There was only Sister Patricia who was Irish."

SISTER PATRICIA: They were not supposed to speak their own language which was kind of hard when you think of it now. But some children came to school they didn't know a word of English. You had to begin from scratch with them. But you'd be surprised at how fast they would pick up. Very fast. They spoke English but always there was a lot of Indian you know. When they thought they were not heard they'd talk Indian, naturally. But the Chilcotin were the worst for that. They knew no English at all when they came. Because you see the parents were never at school and they didn't know English, especially the mothers. The others, a lot of their parents had been in school and some of their grandparents were in school. It made a big difference. The newcomers — with some exceptions of course — they were able to do their grade one in a year. Now of course they really worked. There was not a minute lost in school. And you didn't have to be getting after them you know. Once the work was given that was it. They wanted to do it.

You know the mission ranch, I suppose there are thousands of acres, very big. They grew everything that they used, like vegetables. It was abundant of everything. Then they had a lot of cattle on the ranch. The ranch supported the school to a great extent. It would be hard to make ends meet otherwise because there was very little money coming from the government. I think they allowed a dollar a day for each pupil, and all to feed them and dress them and teach them, look after their health . . . it was so little. The teachers or those working in the school they could have very small salaries. And you couldn't expect it because it would be impossible. Well of course we were missionaries and we were not working for money. Well we got a small allowance, I never bothered about how much it was, but I know everybody was working hard and they didn't expect much for it.

There were always as many children as we could accept. As far as possible they took in as many as they could every year. Some were graduated and then they'd take as many more in as left, as many as they had a bed for. And they had to be a least six or seven, except it would be an orphan; they'd take them younger. But then in holiday time they'd go with the others. The Indians were good that way. If the child didn't have his parents or a real home they'd take him and let him go with their children during the holiday.

David and Celestine Johnson remember one small Indian child, "She's that little girl that Sister Euphrasia adopted. Kind of a baby, 'bout three years. The Sister adopted her and she's named by her. I think her name is Helena 'Phrasia, but then kids call her Euphrasia. She's from Soda Creek, they call her Helena. The Sister, that's her godmother."

SISTER PATRICIA: Sometimes some of the children would run away. They might take that idea overnight, and they'd have no reason. When they were asked why they went, they said "We just wanted to go." They don't think of anything that will follow, or that they'll have to come back, that they may get punished. Some never reached their home. They'd be caught before they'd get there. Some did, then of course the parents knew that it was their duty to bring them back. They watched the opportunity. Some said that they heard their people were sick. Others would say they got lonesome. Very light pretences. Oh it was queer. And they'd never be so nice as before they would run away. Sometimes when they'd be extra nice, we'd say "Something's going to happen." And sure enough there'd be two or three gone. Nobody saw them going.

Now one time there was a number of children sick. They'd a kind of flu. White ladies from Williams Lake came out and they really helped. They cooked and they helped in nursing and everything. They used to go out every day for quite a while to help out the Sisters because they knew how it was when you had maybe sixty or eighty children in bed and the rest of the place to keep going. There was every kind of those children's diseases, measles and whooping cough, anything like that, or then they'd take bad colds or pneumonia. I remember the only doctor was at Quesnel, and Quesnel was a good bit from the mission. It was 75 miles at least. So you had to be really sick to have a doctor come around. It was a good few years at the mission the priests were buying drugs, all kinds of bandages, all kinds of salve, aspirins. Then, later on, the government supplied them. Now when newcomers would come the doctor would come in the fall and vaccinate them and that but all other care was done at the school. Well the children were more healthy than they are now with all the modern care. Oh much more! Outside of the odd epidemic there was hardly anybody in bed although it was so cold.

During the flu of 1918, everybody around had the flu. Hundreds of people died and nobody at the mission took it. Not a soul! And the priests were going out to the dying and the sick — there was Father Thomas and Father Maillard — and they didn't bring it in with them. It was miraculous. They attributed it to St. Joseph. They were praying to St. Joseph because it was St. Joseph's Mission, but nobody at the mission took the flu. They didn't allow people to come in either. They had to phone if they needed the priest. At Sugar Cane reserve they died by the hundreds. And the white people were dying. That was an awful time. And it was very contagious. The priests were out very often.

In later years things began to get better. The children went out more. They went out to ball games and they were more mixed up with the white children. And then some white people from Williams Lake were very interested in the school too. The children were very good at art. They were real artists some of them and then if the whites, especially the ladies, heard about this some of them would be interested in coming. They all appreciated the school and they appreciated the work that was done at the school. They were

A view of the girls' school and convent at St. Joseph's Mission. (John Brioux, OMI).

always in admiration because it meant a lot you know. It meant a lot of work for those at the head to keep everything going.

In 1923, Sister Patricia was transferred to LeJacq Indian School near Fraser Lake, a large, new establishment with modern conveniences that had replaced the log Indian school at Stuart Lake. The school took in children from Stuart Lake, Fort St. James, Stoney Creek, Fort Fraser (Knockley), Steilacoom Reserve, Lower Post, Telegraph Creek, Burns Lake, and Hazelton. Commenting on the children at the school, Sister Patricia remarked, "I suppose for them it must have been hard because they were use to be home. But to have their freedom, even if they have much less of anything else, they would go for the freedom." Sister Patricia remained at LeJacq for 12 years.

SISTER PATRICIA: I went back to Sechelt in 1935. I was there for six years at that time, and I had care of the medicine. Lots of Indians were coming to the school there to get their drugs. If they wanted aspirins or pills for this or that well, drugs that were not dangerous of course, they were dispensed at the school. So that brought all the Indians. Every day or every other day, there'd be somebody wanting something, so I got to know a lot of them like that, because I had to water a lot of stuff. We got it in big half-gallon or gallon bottles and it had to be put in four-ounce bottles, or eight-ounce bottles or whatever. It was quite a work.

The Indians were far more advanced. The women were talking English. There was still a lot of them going to church. I wouldn't say they were all going, but a lot. Now the drink brought trouble. This leaked in and when that begins it's their downfall. They've no resistance whatever. So anybody that has any money at all it would go on that. They were not continually drinking because they couldn't. They had to go out and work. The men were doing a lot of logging. They had to go off and spend weeks away from Sechelt, logging. Fishing then was a great industry. They'd go up to Jervis Inlet, there was a river up there and the Sechelt Indians were going there and they'd stay the whole fishing season up there. The whole family would move. And that was to make money to live on during the winter. They were quite well-off because they were working like this. There was just the old people stayed in the village and the smaller children.

When I went back in the thirties' lots of the young Indians, especially the girls, were coming to pick fruit and the hops. The hop-picking, that was a big thing. Well there you meet all kinds of people so they lost a lot at this. They made a lot of money but they lost a lot of their good qualities. The priests didn't like when they were coming out to the hop fields because they knew what was going on. They lived in shacks or tents. When they got involved with the whites, they didn't get involved with the good whites. At school they were prepared for all this; they were prepared for the dangers they would meet. Archbishop Duke used to say — every place he went to give Confirmation, the white parishes too — "the people who know their faith well are the Indians." I remember him telling that to the whites around here.

The school gave them everything they have now as far as education and they got their religion with the missionaries. That's the work of the missionaries the work of Our Lord, to go and teach the Gospel to *all* nations of the world. They were pagans. They were simple pagans. But if you want to live the way our nature would tell you to live, certainly the Commandments would be an embarrassment for you. And to learn that if you break those Commandments you sin, this would be very . . . wouldn't be pleasant for those people to hear. They'll take God's favours, lots of fish, lots of good game for hunting, you know — "We own all the land around we can fish as much as we like but don't talk to me about not doing what I like" — or don't talk to them about making a sacrifice like to get up and go to church, or say a few prayers in the morning or in the evening.

The Indians would have learned English from their intercourse with the white people even if there was never a school. They did! The Indian men, who were never at school, all could talk English, because they were working with white men who spoke only English. They knew all the bad words in English too. I never met an Indian man yet who couldn't talk English — some more or less well — but they understood and they could talk it. The women were not so keen because they were not going out and they were not meeting. The children would have learned English. And if they had gone to a white school — do you think that they were going to teach them in Indian? What teacher in a white school can talk Indian? The missionaries learned Indian and could speak it fluently and translated everything into Indian. They'd even Indian dictionaries. What teacher would do that today? They never taught them anything about religion that they didn't understand in their own language.

They wanted them to speak English because they had to do their schooling in English. What good was Indian? It was a dialect, it wasn't really a language so to speak. It was not in the commercial world. Each tribe has a different language. Well, how would that work? They couldn't live all their lives like that. Sechelt tribe was a different language than that down here. They had to communicate with people who spoke other languages. They were very keen on their English. Their grandparents and I suppose their parents too

always spoke Indian. They could always have kept it up if they wanted to. When they went home nobody told them to speak English. White children now, they do their reading in English, well if they're French-Canadians when they're home they'll talk French with their parents. Up at LeJacq they used to pray one week in Indian, one week in English. It was a written language. There were prayer books . . . and the Sisters at LeJacq learned the prayers in Indian and the hymns, and they sang them with them. And the priests were preaching in English in the reserves and there was an Indian man translating it. It showed he knew it in English if he could translate it, and he was quite fast too.

When asked if she remembered Sister Patricia, Celestine Johnson remarked, "I really knew Sister Patricia. I liked her, she was a nice Sister. Once she tried to get mad at us, we talked to her 'till she laughed! She was nice." Asked if she was satisfied with her life as a missionary, Sister Patricia replied, "I never regretted coming out. I had a very happy life."

Opposite: Sister Patricia is in the centre, back row, of this portrait of missionaries, nuns, and children of St. Joseph's Mission, circa 1923. (Sister Patricia).

AN INDIAN REMEMBERS

Mary Englund was born in Lillooet, the home of her mother's people, in 1904. Her father, a French-Canadian, named her Marie Anne. Until she was about six years old the family lived at what is now Bralorne, approximately 35 miles west of Lillooet, but when her father died in 1910 the family returned to the Indian reserve. An older brother and two sisters had attended and left the Indian residential school at Mission before Mary and a younger brother were taken there in 1912. The school was run by the Oblates who had charge of the boys, while the Sisters of St. Ann had charge of the girls. Mary has strong memories of her school days; some things she remembers with pleasure, some she recalls with bitterness. Still a faithful Catholic and lay spiritual leader, she is nevertheless quite candid about her school experiences.

MARY ENGLUND: By this time [1912] we were old enough — my brother and myself — to go to the boarding school. There was no school around so the priests used to come and collect the children to go to school like from Fountain and Lillooet and Bridge River and all around. That was Father Rohr and Father Chirouse and all those. They'd come around once or twice a year and they'd count out the children and take stock I guess you might as well say. And then they would say when you were ready to go to school. Your parents had to supply you with clothes such as shoes, underwears and before that, when my older sisters and brother went to the school, they had to have blankets and sheets and everything. So mother figured since she already supplied all that, that would be there so we didn't have to take any. So the priest said we didn't have to take any, just our clothes. But even at that our clothes were pretty skimpy.

Life was tough. It wasn't very nice, you see, because my mother was alone. My grandmother really kind of kept an eye on us, looked after us and kept us together. Because mother had to go out and work. However, we managed to get along. There was my uncle, then there was my grandmother, you see we all lived in the village. We each had our own house but everybody took care of one another. If grandmother wasn't around my uncle who was the chief then he took care of us. Everybody looked after one another more or less. Of course mother was home a good part of the time but there was times she had to leave us otherwise we never got anything to eat.

Father Chirouse picked us up when the train came to Lillooet. I was really excited, because we'd never been anywhere outside of going here and there to one reserve and another either in a canoe or boat and on horseback. It was something really exciting to go on the train. We were left alone so many times we never had the tendency to say, "Well, I'm sorry I'm going to go away and leave my mother" because we were alone most of the time. And I couldn't

Opposite: Mary Englund at her home in Lillooet. Photograph by Alex Morris, OMI. (Alex Morris).

understand why they were cryin'. My brother and I, we enjoyed it you know. We enjoyed the train ride as far as that went. It was fun. It was something new. It was the old steam engines. Father Chirouse was the one that took us. He was awfully nice. I remember he talked to us and then he'd go further and get in the other seats and we'd look over to see what he's doing. We were able to open the windows and look out to see what we were passing. It was really fascinating until we got to Squamish and then we had to go on a boat and by this time it was dark. After we got to Vancouver I remember walking along the street with *big buildings* — fascinating — we couldn't understand all these big buildings. Finally we got on another train and we finally got to Mission. And then we had to walk. I thought we'd *never* get there.

Then I had to leave my brother. I couldn't understand why I had to leave him in this other building while I went to the other building. You see there was a big building where the boys lived, and then you went along and there was a big church, and then you went along and that's where the girls lived. These were three-storey buildings. There was the main floor and the second floor and on the third floor we slept, all the girls slept. And I remember when I got there I couldn't figure out why I had to leave my brother . . . and I kept asking but they said that he had to stay with the rest of the boys. I wanted to know why.

I had never seen a nun in my life. So these people with their covered up heads and white around and then their black robes and black veil — how the Sisters of St. Ann dressed — I couldn't figure out why they had to wear such clothes. And I used to ask the girls, "Why's she dressed like that?" "Because she's a Sister." "Well, what's a Sister?" They told us we had to stay there for a whole year, well I didn't know what a year was. That was the other problem, "When's the year going to end?"

So anyway this one big girl — she'd been there quite a while — she took me over to this other building. Way at the back of the convent was another big building where they did all the washing and you did your bath and there were

A group of Lillooet Indians, 1867–68. Photograph by Frederick Dally.
(BCPM, Ethnology Division, photo no. PN 1425).

square wooden tubs. You heat the water and you filled it and that's where you had to have your bath. You didn't go to bed — when you first got there — without your bath. Every girl that came in they had to be taken to the laundry and put through the wash. And then you had to take all your clothes off and leave them there and then they gave you other clothes to put on. Sort of a uniform. They were white blouses, they buttoned at the back and there was a sort of a jumper with frills around the sleeves and buttoned at the back — 'course I couldn't button them so I had to have somebody to help me — and underwears and long black stockings and underwears down to the ankle and then the black stockings over it. Oh my! It didn't please me. I very seldom had these big longjohns on — I would call them now, long underwear — and then these big black stockings on, because at home we never wore any of those things. We had little panties on down to the knees with little frills around and I couldn't figure out these long things and then these stockings over. And then we had to have garters to hold them up. Then black shoes with little high-top laces . . . the only shoes I had were boys' lecky boots in those days and I thought, "Oh boy I was dressed up." Because we at home hardly ever wore any shoes. We wore moccasins and we ran all summer bare-footed. I really was uncomfortable. But they were handy when it came cold.

But oh my was I *ever* homesick. You know home wasn't much, in fact the nuns didn't call it home, they called it our *camp*. And that used to hurt me. It still does when I think about it. When we'd talk about going home they'd say, "You're not going home you're going back to your camp." That was their impression of the reserve. Well in a way they were right because the homes we had in those days were made out of great big log houses. And the house we got into didn't even have a floor in it. It was just dirt floor. Then we used to have to every so often go out and chop boughs and put them on the floor to keep the dust down, until mother was able to get some lumber and put the floor down. You know we were raised in a hard way, so going to school and going in the convent it was very unusual.

This one girl she was very good to me. Apparently she had come from the same reserve I did but I don't ever remember her. So anyway she was awfully good with me. She helped me in the mornings to dress. We were given a basin and a towel, tooth-powder and toothbrush and a comb. That was ours. We had little squares in the washroom and the washroom was quite a length and all window in front so the Sister could look in from the dormitory. And this great big galvanized trough with the cold water, cold taps, and in there were the basins. You filled up your basin then you went over to the counter — no hot water, all cold water — then you had to scrub your teeth in the sink, then you had to wash your basin and put it underneath the counter. You had to fold up your towel and take it with you and put it at the head of your bed. And there was squares for your comb and your toothbrush and tooth-powder. So that was our gadgets.

An older girl saw to it that you were dressed. Then of course it took us time to put on these long stockings and high boots, and laces. And your hair had to be braided at the back and put up in a nob. You couldn't have one little hair hanging on your face. It had to be smoothed back. So she used to help me comb my hair. She'd wet my hair and comb it and braid it here and braid it there, then she'd braid it at the back and roll it up and pin it up. That was the way we were supposed to have our hair. At home we got up, washed our face and we didn't think of combing our hair; we just took it and tied it up and that was it.

We lived a simple life you know and then to go into these places where we didn't know that we didn't have to talk. That was another big thing. Everything was *silent*. You lived by the bell. The bell rang you shut up. Not another word. And here we'd keep on talking, us that were new, and we had to be shushed and shaken and what-not. Then we had to go in lines you see, one behind the other, go upstairs. No matter where you went you were in line. You never moved until the bell rang. There was a little bell always, no matter where you went. Or one of those desk push-bells.

I never forget that night when we first went there. We were outside in the yard and this bell rang inside. I said, "What's that for?" "Oh come on, come on. We've got to go for supper." So away we went and had supper. We got in there. "Don't talk, don't talk. No, don't talk just get in line. No, not one word." And then we went into the dining room and they put us in certain places and then the grace was said. The bell rang, then you sat down. Great big long tables — there must be 20 on each table — and the benches and galvanized plates — or tin plates as we called them — the same with saucers. And we had a fork and a spoon. There was never much of knives because you didn't get no butter and you didn't get no meat to cut up; everything was grounded up. And green tea. We never got no milk except skim milk to put in your tea. Of course me — I was not knowing the rules — I was talking to this girl who was with me. She told me what to do, "You don't talk before the bell rings and you don't talk after the bell rings either." So we kept on talking, the bell was ringing and we were still talking and she'd come over and shush me up.

'Course the Sisters were pretty good in a way too you know. If they knew you were new and didn't know the rules they'd say, "Here! You remember now you're not supposed to talk after the bell rings?" I remember this one Sister, her name was Sister "V," she'd great big eyes you know. She was a French nun. My she was *miserable*. She'd roll her eyes around. Gosh we had to watch for her. This Sister "V" was a real needle in the side and you know the Indians they have a name for everything and the owl always has a big eye you know and so this nun we all called her chkilulek, the owl.

You got up around five-thirty in the morning. The bell rings and you had to get up. You had to go and wash and dress and get your hair combed and make your little — we had little cots and the mattresses were full of straw — and you had to make your bed, make it really neat. You can't just slip-slop, everything had to be tight. If you didn't make your bed right the nun would come along and pull all the sheets and blankets off and you had to make it over. You had to fold up your nightgown and put it under your pillow. You had a little closet to hang your clothes in. If those weren't neat in there you either had to kneel down somewhere in some corner or kept silent at the dining room meal time.

After breakfast each one had their offices to go to. They called them offices, that was jobs. A certain amount of girls went to the dormitory, they had to put white spreads on the beds. A certain amount of girls went to the kitchen, a certain amount of girls stayed in the dining room and washed the dishes. See there was 51 girls and there was certain ones that swept the halls and cleaned the halls. My first job was in the classroom. I went with these two big girls to go to the classrooms; they were to clear the classroom out. There was one classroom and we had shifts. The middle ones went to school in the morning, the big girls went to the sewing room. We had to clean the boards, clear the brushes and dust everything, dust the desks and swept the floors. So this was where I had my first experience that you were not to touch a nun.

This one girl, she was an older girl — 'course most of the time I didn't know what to do so I just stood around and helped move the desks once in a while — she took this brush and she laid them alongside the windowsill and you could see down to the street from where our classroom was. I didn't put them there. She must have. When the teacher — she was a nun — came in and saw these brushes on the window ledge she wanted to know who put them there. And of course the other girl didn't want to get into trouble so she said I did. I said, "I didn't!" Oh, I was determined I wasn't going to be told that I did it. So the nun came up to me and she kind of tapped me on the face. She said, "Did you put the brushes on the windowsill?" "No, I didn't." I pushed her. She pretty near went over the desk. She could have hurt herself very badly. But how was I to know I wasn't to touch her? She was supposed to be something precious that you can't lay your hand on. So anyhow she left me alone and I cried all morning, didn't do my work. And that was another thing, I couldn't talk at dinnertime. That was my punishment. So this girl she told me we were not to touch the Sisters. "Well," I said, "she slapped me!" Oh I wasn't going to be slapped. That smoothed over after that I remember, and I told the Sister that I did not put those brushes on the window ledge. But you see when you're new they take advantage of you.

Everybody went to catechism eight thirty in the morning until nine and then there was school. The older girls went to the sewing room and they mended socks and underwear and whatever there had to be mended and that's where I made my first encounter with a nun too. She would give us those long black stockings — sometimes they wore off on the heel or the toe — and you'd stick your hand in there and they'd give you a darning needle and you'd mend them, darn them in other words. I didn't want to darn in one place because it was thin, so I just mended the hole and that was it. We had to go and show them to the Sister when we had finished and she'd stick her hands in the sock and work her finger out. If her finger went through it was just too bad. You had to do it over again. She put her finger through my sock and I don't know what I said to her but she got really annoyed at me. She says, "Now stick your hand out." She had great big scissors and she hit me. I was really annoyed. I didn't cry at first and she looked at me and I don't know what she saw in my face but I know she looked terrible to me. I went and sat down and I banged down. You know how you do when you get mad. She says, "Come back here. You kneel right there and finish your sock." On my knees! I didn't have no thread in my needle so I just sat there and sucked my needle.

But later on when I got a little higher and a little older I used to go to the sewing room in the morning and she started teaching us how to run the machines and sew. First it was aprons — we all had to wear aprons — so she gave me this material she cut it out — she never let us cut it out — and then she showed us where to sew and your stiching had to be straight. So I started this zig zag. She'd make me rip it over and I'd sit there and cry and rip, and the names I didn't call her. 'Course to myself. It never came out because I didn't dare. I didn't trust nobody; you couldn't in a convent you know. You'd say one thing and this girl might go and tell Sister and you got punished for it so you had to say things to yourself that you didn't like.

We weren't allowed to speak our language in school. We had to speak English right from day one. I was pretty well bilingual you might as well say. When we first moved to the reserve we couldn't talk Indian either. We had to learn from the kids we played with and during this time while we were on the reserve we kept pretty well, at least I did, to our language and we talked in

Indian girls leaving the church at St. Mary's Mission, circa 1913. (Mary Englund).

Indian too. So it didn't bother me too much although it was kind of different and you got mixed up. It was a difficult situation. See they had different Indian dialects. Along the Fraser Valley they had the Stalo and the Thompson and us here was the Chehalis. We talked differently than they did. So if we talked to them it was all English. Even if we could talk with one another, the nuns wouldn't allow it. Of course there was a lot of us that could talk the same language; you take from Fountain to Pavillion down to Mount Currie we all talked same language. When we were alone in some corner we did talk our own language and if the Sister caught us it was, "You talk English!" That's where a lot of girls kind of forgot their language. If you're there, stayed there a certain length of the time, you forget certain words in Indian. You couldn't explain yourself too much in Indian as you would in English. They said it was better for us to speak English because we could learn English and read and write better if we kept our English, if we spoke English instead of talking Indian.

When the principal came over — Father Rohr; he was French — they'd sit and talk French and we knew very well they was talking about us, all of us, and we resented that very much. They wouldn't allow us to talk Indian but they could talk French. We used to tell them that, "How come you can talk in French in front of us and you wouldn't allow us to talk Indian in front of you?" And of course they got after us for that. You weren't allowed to question. Oh yes, they weren't very nice in that respect.

Of course all the parents thought that was great you see, that we should talk English and be able to write so that we'd be able to write letters when we got home, to do things for the Indian people. You were something great when you come home, "Oh she can write now." They were kind of proud of us in a way once you were able to write your name, your mother's name, your father's name and whoever was in the family. We were doing all right. They were proud of you then. I remember my grandmother — I don't know how old she was but she was partly blind and she was all crippled with arthritis — she'd pat us on the head because we can write.

We were not to tell our parents what went on in the school. That was another rule. We were not allowed to discuss what goes on in school when we go home. We never got sugar at school, no sugar in our porridge or in our tea so when we went home I guess this one girl was telling her parents how she never got sugar at school. When she got back to school she was really reprimanded by the principal Father Rohr. And he didn't go about it in a nice way. He went about it in a way very insulting, telling you what you did in your *camp* and what you told your father and mother and the tattletales. And your parents never had anything to say of what you were doing in the school because they didn't know. I was told I was not to tell my mother of what went on. Whatever we did outside the school when we went home, if it wasn't just what it should be, we heard about it when we got back to the school. We were punished for it. If the girls that went to school with you saw you in the village with so and so, if they had anything against you or felt jealous of you in anyway, they'd tell the Sister and you'd get reprimanded for it. But I was lucky, there was nobody else from my village, just me.

But you didn't dare rebel, whatever they said was gospel. There was two girls that got dismissed while I was there. That was a terrible thing. I don't know, sometime in September or October I think it was they ran away from school. We were staying up quite late that evening until 9 o'clock. We were having games and so on and all at once these girls disappeared. And come line-up time to get ready to go to bed they weren't there. Boy that was terrible for us. We were concerned you know. So anyway we went to bed. We thought maybe they're just hiding downstairs somewhere. And once you go to bed, once you get up in the dormitory there's a trapdoor that goes over the stairs and that's got a great big bolt that Sister puts in there. Nobody can get through there. So you were locked up there. I often think afterwards, when I got older, what would we do if the bottom part of the building got burnt? How would we get out of there? But anyway they were brought back about a month or so later on. They were found and brought back and their parents were notified. And they really got reprimanded. They not only got reprimanded I remember they went to bed one evening and there was one big husky Sister, she came up and she had a great big — you know they used to use the razor straps for shaving? Well she had one of those with a wooden handle on it. They laid on their stomach on the bed and they really went to work on them. I don't know how many straps they got but we were all crying, everybody was sniffling and crying. That strap was used on very serious occasions

They gave you notes. Like in school you have certain notes, if it's "A" you're perfect, "B" you're not too good, "C" you're gettin' worse and "D" you're very poor and you need reprimanding and you need the strap or something. I lost my note, this was really funny, I was working in the kitchen. I used to work in the pantry helping the Sister. She was grinding up this meat to make meatballs for *their* table — they had a dining room by themselves — so I cleaned up the meat grinder. 'Course I had scraps of meat left and I came down into the kitchen. Sister was French, she could hardly talk English. There was a pot of hash on the stove for the girls, ground up meat and potatoes and everything was in that big pot of hash, so I went and I asked her what was I to do with this handful of scraps of meat. Instead of saying "hash" she said, "Put it in your ass." And I started to laugh, and oh she was annoyed at me. She went right away and told Sister Superior and of course I lost my note for that. We were reprimanded because we're not to condemn the nuns because they couldn't speak very good English and they reminded us that we weren't perfect in English either because we spoke Indian.

Every occasion that comes up like a principal's birthday, like Father Rohr's birthday, or he'd go away and he'd come back and we'd have a welcoming party, and the Sister would write out a speech and you had to read that to the priest. And there was always somebody to read that big speech, you had to read this in long sheets you know and you had to read *every word perfect*. I read it several times but my cousin she was always getting chosen to read this, and you had to practise that. You had to practically memorize it in order to make a perfect recitation. Sister "V" would say, "Now if you weren't an Indian girl you could do that perfectly well, better; a white girl she would go over that very well, nicely."

They were always degrading us because we were Indian. We didn't come from homes we came from *camps* and we didn't know how to live. We ate rotten fish so they didn't seem to be particular in what they gave us to eat. They never let us forget that we were *Indian,* and that we weren't very civilized, that we were more or less savages. The other nuns weren't too forward with their mentioning of Indians, but this particular nun, Sister "V," she looked after us in the recreation room and she looked after us in the dining room — once in a while the other nun would come and take her place — and she looked after us in the dormitory. She was constantly with us, which I think was too much of a strain for her. If they had changed places I think it would have eased her tension a little more and she wouldn't have been so hateful towards us.

There was a couple of Sisters that really showed their affection. One was Sister Mary André. Whenever I met her in the hall she'd put her arms around me and she really showed that she was a happy-go-lucky person. And then there was our teacher, Sister Mary Hildegard. You were privileged if you could go down town with the Sisters, if they had something to do down town, to go and mail letters or go and pay bills and you were privileged if you were chosen to go with the Sister. We'd go down town and you see you were not to touch them but the minute we got outside the door and out the yard she'd hold my hand. Oh it was really a privilege.

Most of them were pretty nice. Like our teacher, she was pretty nice but we were told that we were expected to stand up and if we didn't she used to report us to Sister Superior. We were called rude if we didn't stand up whenever any of them entered. Same way if you passed them in the hall or anywhere, you're to stop and bow your head. They were really up on the pedestal. I guess it was good training in a way. I don't know. They sure put themselves somewhere where you couldn't touch them. You couldn't reach them and you had to bow to them, that's something I could never . . . it made me to a certain extent very bitter by the time I left school.

Another thing that made me very rebellious was the punishment. They used prayer to punish you. If you were late or you disobeyed in one way or another you knelt down and you said 10 Hail Marys or 10 Our Fathers or something like that. Well saying these things was against your nature. You know it wasn't a praying thing and therefore I rebelled against it. I couldn't see the sense of using prayer as a punishment.

And going in the chapel you couldn't look at the next person. We wore veils and we went in there with our hands folded and even if we nudged there's a nun watching way at the back and she saw everything that went on. You got your ears pulled or you got a slap in the face. On special occasions we wore great big veils that came down. You wore that and you had uniforms to go with that, and we thought that was great to wear a great big long veil. You were an angel or something. They were pinned in our hair and they had to stay there. But I guess it was a way of teaching you respect. You were not to look around but there were little instances as you came in the church, because the boys sat on one side and we sat on the other. It got so the older girls, the minute you'd come in a certain boy would cough and of course some girl would answer. Finally the nuns would catch on, "Who was that that did that?" and of course nobody didn't dare tell. No, you were a tattletale if you told. You were not to talk to a boy unless it was your brother. And you were not to have any way of showing any kind of signs or anything to a boy.

I tell you one instance. The boys were cleaning the eaves. They'd get full of moss and they were cleaning and there was great big long ladders put up and this one ladder was left at the end of the building and that was going into the lavatories. And the windows were able to be opened, screens could be taken off and opened. Apparently a bunch of the boys had decided that they were going to go over to the convent and raid the girls' dormitory. I think there was four or five of them, quite big boys, and they got into the dormitory about midnight by using the ladder. The dormitory, sleeping 50 girls, is quite a large place and away in one corner the nun slept. She had her little caboose, we called it, a walled-off room. And they got down the middle of the dormitory and they were waking some of the girls up. In those days, when you're young, you're scared of anything in the dark. 'Course there was dim lights all over the dormitory but you couldn't see very well. One of the girls, she was so scared she crawled on the floor and went and knocked on the nun's door. This one boy he was trying to crawl in bed with one of the girls and she was trying to push him off the bed, and then the nun came out and they all took off — down through the ladder again. One boy he was still in the middle of the dormitory and they had blackened their faces so they wouldn't be seen. We were all talking because the Sister had gone downstairs to tell Sister Superior and all at once, as we looked up, this black thing came up at the foot of my bed. I hollered and I pulled my blanket and my feet were stickin' out! He went downstairs. I don't know how he got out but he went downstairs. We had a new Father Superior by this time and they got a strapping and the girls of course they got blamed for enticing the boys to come over. Some of the girls apparently were getting familiar with the boys, so they decided they were going to go and visit the girls. You could call them gutsy.

When you went home you missed the companionship of the others. You felt alone. Although the family was there, my brothers were there, my older brother, my uncle, my grandmother — we always had an uncle live with us because he was blind — but you were lonely. At least I was, and children on the reserve were not of your . . . oh they were *people* you know, but they weren't like the ones you had in the convent. So it was different. You talked to them, they were nice to you, they wanted to know what the school was all about. And we'd go swimming. Things were different but mother always tried to make life easier for us. She always had a garden. We'd weed the garden and then when we got through the horses were saddled and we packed up lunch and we went up in the hills picking berries. We spent our holiday that way. We'd come down and then we'd get ready before we went back to school. There was washing and ironing and getting ready and bathing and hair-washing. Then we'd hit the train. We never felt that we were leaving somebody that we loved. We were glad to get away. Wasn't that something? We were anxious to get on that train; we were anxious to be on our way. We never thought that well maybe we should say good-bye to mother she'll feel bad.

She died while I was in school. But then we weren't allowed . . . once you had no parents, there was no home to go to, you weren't allowed out of the school. I wasn't allowed out anyway. My younger brother and myself, we stayed in the school. We did have family at home, but after my mother died we weren't allowed to go home. We weren't even allowed to go to the funeral, which hurt me very much because I was old enough to understand. So there I was kind of left with my two brothers to look out for. My one brother was two years younger than me and the little one he was just about eight or nine years old.

Mary Englund on the grounds of St. Mary's Mission, circa 1920. (Mary Englund).

I wanted to be a nun and I spoke to them about it, but you see your father and mother had to be married and you had to produce their marriage certificate and you had to have a certain amount of money, otherwise it was useless. You might as well go talk to the wall. I wanted very much to be a nun. Sister Bernadette, she was our Mother Superior there for a while, I told her. So she says, "You know you can't get married, you can't have children?" I said I didn't want any, I wanted to be a nun. I was about 15 then. She says, "Did you know your father and mother have to be married in the Church?" which they weren't. She says, "You'll need money you know." I didn't have no money. I never even got money from home at times. I didn't, that was another thing that I rebelled very much against. For money and because my father and mother weren't married I couldn't join, but I still had that desire to become a nun.

I was there for just two years after, I was about 16 then, when the principal came over one day. He thought I had gone as far as I could go. In those days the grades weren't as high as the public schools were. If you were in grades five and six you were equal to grades eight and 10 in the public schools and I was in grade six. I could have gone to high school or finished school anywhere but I wasn't allowed to because that's as high as I was going to go, that's high as *Indian* girls went. You worked around the convent if you stayed there. You did the cooking, you did the washing, you did the supervising if you wanted to stay at the convent. You didn't get paid for it though.

We'd got a new principal by this time, his name was Father Duplanil and him and Father Hartmann came over one day and they said, "You're no good to the school anymore and you can't go any higher so you may as well go out. There's a lady in Ladner that would like a girl to keep house for her. She'll teach you how to cook. She'll look after you." She was 83 years old and she was a well-to-do woman. So they took me down there. I didn't know what I was getting into. The money was more fascinating to me because I knew I'd have money to be able to do something with my brothers, to be able to buy them nice clothes and I would be able to buy nice clothes. I was told I'd get $35 a month, oh it was big money in those days, but I never did. I never got no more than $20 a month. It was just to get me there you see. And I used to cry. Because Ladner was worlds away from where I'd been. And being with a bunch of girls all these years, well pretty near 10 years, and then to go and live with this cranky old woman was just ridiculous. And she was more strict than the nuns were.

She was Scotch. She had high blood pressure and she had arthritis. She couldn't walk properly, and you had to wait on her hand and foot. I was there for a year and she took sick. She had pneumonia and pleurisy and the doctor used to come from Vancouver and she had trained nurses to come look after her and she was so miserable they didn't last. One lasted three days and another lasted three or four days and she took off. So I had to do all the work, looking after her. I'd sit up all night. She had a kettle by her bed with Friar's Balsam in it and I had to keep that filled and I'd sit by her bed all night long. Very little sleep. It got towards spring I took sick so when the doctor came over he ordered me out of there — Ladner's very damp — so he told me to go to a drier climate for two or three weeks. Well I came up here and I never went back. She sent the two priests after me but I told them I'd go back next week but I never did go back because that $20 a month didn't seem important to me, my health was more important.

The Sisters of Christ the King building a hen house at their home on Anaham reserve,
circa 1945. (Sister Teresa Bernard).

NEW MISSIONARIES, OLD PROBLEMS

By the late 1920s, the old European missionaries were being replaced by Canadian-born or, at least, Canadian-educated ones. In many cases, their attitude towards their missionary role was more realistic than idealistic. Nevertheless, they were to encounter the same difficulties as their predecessors.

Yet, in spite of abuses by white government, white business interests and white settlers, the Indians continued to seek out and welcome Christianity. In 1927, for example,

CHIEF ROY AZAK: The people of Canyon City start to want for preacher to look after the village. They try the Anglicans, which they belong, but they were turned down for few people. They — the Anglican Church — could not look after them. Tell them to move to other villages where they is already a priest. But the chief said, "There's lots of branches in this religion, we may look for another branch." So the chiefs went down to Prince Rupert and write letter to the Salvation Army. Early in the spring, 1927, about April, they received the word that the Salvation Army officer will be coming up around May.

Given the continued goodwill of the people, the new missionaries could feel confident of great results. Perhaps all that was needed was a new, more realistic approach? The Durieu System, for example, proved to be distasteful to many of the new Catholic missionaries — as it had to some of the old.

FATHER ALEX MORRIS: I studied it during a month or so at the insistence of Father Thomas. By the mid-year I could get along, carry on a conversation in the Chinook jargon, and by that time I was also convinced the Durieu System was for somebody else, not for me. I felt the Durieu System at best might have been good 50 years, 100 years before, but it was useless to the Indians that I was in contact with. The quicker we got away from that type of thing, the sooner we changed the language, the better it would be.

But among the Catholic missionaries changes in the missionary system did not necessarily bring unqualified success. Certainly this proved to be the case among the Chilcotins where, in the 1940s, several changes in regard to missionary activity took place.

As early as the 1870s and 1880s, Paul Durieu, like the Church Missionary Society personnel, had hoped to attract the Indian peoples to the ministry and to the religious orders. In 1947, Archbishop W. M. Duke of Vancouver held the same hope:

69

In order to help Indian people in the Chilcotin country, we induced the Sisters of Christ the King to come to Anaham to open a school in an old Indian Community Hall, which became a school building and the Sisters occupy practically a shack beside it, and began also a Novitiate for Indian girls, the first in Western Canada through which Indian girls would be trained for official workers, teachers and nurses, to work among their own people.*

Regardless of the optimism of the Archbishop, this venture, failed. The Indians desired religion, the missionaries were willing to provide it, yet advancements apparent in other missionary countries — as accounts of new missionaries reveal — failed to materialize among the peoples of British Columbia.

NEW MISSIONARY TO THE SKEENA

MARGARET BOOTH: My father was the Reverend Victor Harold Sansum and he was born in Stroud, Gloustershire in 1892. There were 16 in his family and he was around the fourteenth. He got rather a bad time at home and so he left home all on his own. His father had a brother in Wisconsin and so this 14-year-old boy came out to Wisconsin and stayed with his relatives. The old Aunty there remembered him. She said, "We could see he was very intelligent and that he was so eager to learn. And he hadn't had much schooling in England — I guess he had to help in his father's store — so we urged him to go to Toronto and get his high school." There were some relatives in Toronto.

While he was in Toronto he had a Sunday school teacher who kind of befriended him, and he took a real shine to her. He wasn't a church person, I don't think he was anything particularly. His family was not Church of England. Sansum is a very unusual name and going back to try and find the history of that I found out they were Hugenots driven out of France because of persecution by the Catholics. That's how I know they were a Protestant family from way back.

He had this Sunday school teacher and she apparently moved to Duncan, British Columbia, and urged him to come west. He enroled in Columbian College in New Westminster. He was a student minister and — from what I can gather — he must have gone to Port Simpson, around 1911, as a student under Dr. Reilly. Then the war came along. He joined up from New Westminster and was with the 47th Battalion. While he was overseas in France he was wounded. When he got a leave and got back to England he went down to Brighton and he met this girl who came out in 1919 as a war bride.

He had a church at Edmonds Street out in Burnaby and he got his BA at UBC. He was also out at Slocan for a while. He liked the outdoor life. He didn't like city life. And having been to Port Simpson I think there was an appeal of the north for him. The Reverend Peter Kelly — he and my dad were classmates — he was Haida, and he may have had some influence in my dad going up to do this mission work. My dad would be *called* you know. You'll see — as the pattern emerges — he keeps going back to the native people rather than working with whites. He seemed to have an empathy for the native people.

* Archbishop William M. Duke to Senator S. McKeen, Ottawa, February 17, 1948. (By courtesy of William Christie.)

Victor Sansum (centre, back row) stands with Indian students from the Port Simpson area. (Mrs. Margaret Booth).

Reverend Sansum went back to the Skeena country in 1923. After a year spent among white parishioners, he transferred to the Indian mission at Kispiox where he remained for three years. In 1927, the family, concerned about the children's lack of education, returned to Vancouver, to Douglas Park United Church. A year later Victor Sansum received his MA from UBC. But, as his daughter put it, "He just seemed to get tired of the city people, and the smallness and pettyness in some of the church work. He had all this education — he tutored in Greek and Hebrew — but he wasn't used to the tea-parties and the visiting." In 1930, Victor Sansum returned to Indian mission work at Port Simpson where the family remained until the death of Mrs. Sansum.

MARGARET BOOTH: We followed the Tomlinsons because I can remember my dad talking about the Tomlinsons being there ahead of us. How much further ahead I don't know. The seeds of Christianity had been sown by the Reverend Tomlinson. Dad had a horse and buggy at that time and he had the various villages to look after as well as Kispiox. He had Kitwancool, Kitwanga and Kitseguecla. We would go around with him to these various villages. The Salvation Army were down in Glen Vowell but there must have been a nucleus of Methodists down in Glen Vowell because my dad would have to go there too.

We lived in a house right beside the church in the middle of the reserve and the totem poles were all around us. There was no running water. We had to pack our water. They had a stone boat with oil drums and my dad had to take this down to the Skeena with a horse. And we cut wood. It must have been very difficult for mother. She came from a very good family in Brighton. Her father was an accountant or something — worked in London. She went to a very exclusive girls' school. And to suddenly come out and be plunged into

this life with no running water and in the middle of an Indian village — in fact I don't think her family ever got over it, that he did this to her.

Our house was a sort of focal point and I can remember hearing sing-songs both in Kispiox and later in Port Simpson. Sunday night singsong. They are very musical, the native people, and he liked music. He played the violin a little bit and he liked to sing. They'd bring their musical instruments and everybody would sing and they would just have the drums, tubas, and all the instruments. I can still see my mother playing the piano and all the Indian people singing all those wonderful old gospel songs. Especially they'd do, "When the roll is called up yonder we'll be there," and booming it out.

He had an interpreter and his name was William Holland. Dad learned a little Chinook — he learnt to speak the language in Port Simpson — he loved languages. Dad could never understand, both with William Holland and the other interpreter he had in Port Simpson — he would say what he had to say but he never actually knew what the interpreter, or how the interpreter, was saying it!

He had a very good working relationship with these people. They were most eager to please him. The Indians were very polite to us, to my dad. There was never any rowing or arguments. The Indians liked the church, liked the music, the service.

They would call my dad, but they would also call the medicine man just to be absolutely sure that things were well taken care of. I can remember Dad mentioning about the medicine man hovering in the wings. One thing I do remember about Kispiox was the beating of the tom toms. Constantly beating. They never stopped. If they ever stopped you wondered, "Why have the

Opposite: William Holland, interpreter for the Reverend Victor Sansum, with his wife Mary and family. (Mrs. Margaret Booth).

Below: The Rev. Victor Sansum and his children, Margaret, Joan and John, beside the Methodist church on Kispiox reserve, 1925. (Mrs. Margaret Booth).

drums stopped?'' These drum beatings were to keep away the evil spirits. We didn't have any of that at Port Simpson. They had progressed.

The one thing that was really hard on him or that he worried about a lot was the potlatching. When there was a potlatch scheduled for the village I can remember him shaking his head and thinking, ''Well I won't be able to do a thing with them for a while,'' because there was so much feasting and carrying on. They always arrived with these white flour sacks 'cause anything they didn't eat — they couldn't eat — they all took home with them.

They'd go on pretty well for a while until another potlatch would come along. I can well remember the despair he had of these potlatches, trying to convince them the error of their ways. They were very generous people. When they threw a potlatch they went into debt to do it and put on a great show. He would go down there to the potlatches and see the ceremonial dances and he would go down and eat with them. They invited him. But it was the alcohol he really despaired of, not the ceremonial part. The drinking affected their personalities.

He realized that their culture was very important to them and he never tried to take that away at all. They realized that he wasn't one to take all this away from them. Same with the totem poles — ''the graven images'' or something — well he didn't try to eradicate that. He would get them to tell him their stories. He was their friend.

REJECTION OF THE DURIEU SYSTEM

FATHER ALEX MORRIS: I was born in Anse-au-Veaufils, Quebec, August 31st, 1911. My father died when I was 11 years old and there were nine in the family. So when I was 12 I quit school — my older brother quit the year before — and we worked at all kinds of things, mostly in two fields, farming and logging, until two of my sisters graduated from the normal school and were teaching. Then I decided I should go and get some education myself.

I had a two-fold vision of the future; both required education. I would either be at sea — but I wanted to be able to get on an officer's rank — I also had some inclination to go into the priesthood. And the priesthood and the sea had an equal sway. The last year of my high school, I applied in February for a job on a boat leaving Montreal for Panama on April fifteenth. I applied with a friend of mine to really make a break from everything and get to sea. But in April the company had gone bankrupt and somebody else had bought the assets and they told us they needed no sailors. So my friend Steve asked, ''What now?'' ''Oh,'' I said, ''there's always the seminary!''

I studied everything about Africa, all of our African missions, the country, the people, the diseases, the bugs, everything. I knew Africa very well by the time I was through at the seminary. So I asked for my first obedience [posting] to be Africa. A member of our General House in Rome said it was impossible for anyone to go to Africa during the war. We had already lost seven priests at sea or in prison camps. I was told to go to British Columbia and work with the Indians for the duration of the war. I couldn't understand myself being a missionary to the Indians. I really didn't know anything about Indians.

Father Morris came to British Columbia in 1942. He was assigned to assist Father Thomas in his work among the Shuswap peoples. Although, as Father Morris discovered, the Shuswaps were now ignoring most aspects of the Durieu

System, Father Thomas insisted that the new missionary learn and continue using the old method. Father Morris spent four years working among Shuswaps and, occasionally, with the Carrier people before he accepted the role of principal of the mission school at Williams Lake.

The new missionary was so "disenchanted" by the work on the Indian reserves that he was prepared to leave the missions; as he observed, "going on any longer was harmful to my health and of no use to the population."

FATHER ALEX MORRIS: They practised a kind of Catholicity which was minimal, which was simple. But I could get along with that because of the simplicity of the people. Because of their daily life they could not be expected to get along with all the complications of the Catholic faith. There was one or two people here and there who had more of a profound faith, but nothing at all to compare with the faith of my ancestors, that I'm thinking about, the people that previous I would have considered having the faith. So I really was not too impressed.

A good number were attending church. A good number were even going to the sacraments. But the process of degeneration of the faith had set in. In some of the villages I know for a fact that Father Thomas went and everybody came to the mission and everybody came to the church and the real attraction was to remain after Father Thomas had gone because as soon as he left there was a whole week of wild parties.

The Durieu System had not worked and was not working. For instance, they used the Durieu System in speaking Chinook language or jargon and having an interpreter interpreting it. But the people all spoke . . . understood the English language — except in the Chilcotin. Father Thomas insisted that I had to speak Chinook to an interpreter. In our missions, English was the language. The prevailing language was the English language. Father Bill Doucey came in 1946 and from the beginning — after he had gone out and studied the problem — he was of the same mind I was. And we both insisted that there was no sense in trying to turn back the clock.

I replaced Jack Hennessy in Alexandria mission when he was teaching at Redstone and I went without an interpreter and I spoke in English. I had met the people and they spoke English. So *I* spoke English. I was there for one weekend — my first check-in there — and when I was about to leave a number of young people came to me and thanked me for having spoken in English to them in church. Before, they would get Chinook and an interpreter interpreted in Carrier and they didn't understand *either* language. They told me they were delighted and they would be back because I was speaking in English and they could understand what I was talking about and what was going on. We learnt Shuswap sufficiently to hear the confession of those who did not speak English. But the great majority came to us, to confession and everything else, in English.

It had been different before. Their own religions were very simple. Animism was as far as you could find out any trace of any. I'm talking about all the history I could find of the Shuswap before the white man came. Everyone that I know of spoke of the sharing; the sharing among the Indians is basically identical to the sharing of the early Christian community. The misunderstanding of land today is based on the sharing of yesterday. You find a deer and whose is it? You come and you share it with everybody. It is the abundance of the earth. It is to be shared. And that was the potlatch. If you

Group celebrating the taking of the habit of two Indian postulants, Sister Miller of Mission and Sister Edward of Pavillion. Group includes Archbishop Duke, centre, and Father Alex Morris, back row, far left. (Sister Teresa Bernard).

accumulated so much you really don't need it through the winter you gave a potlatch and you shared. Your banked wealth is the amount you share with others. The potlatch was a social ritual.

But ritual was also misunderstood by Durieu. Ritual was tradition but he replaced social tradition with Church ritual. For instance at the dance, the dancer asked permission from the chief to dance because of the class his ancestors were in, because of the wars his ancestors had won for the tribe. It was simply historical tradition. That ritual was not in any sense religious format. It was sinful because it was Indian. Even a lullaby was forbidden because it was Indian.

The Durieu System was militaristic. It probably worked for Durieu. In 1920, I would have accepted it myself, because we lived under that system ourselves. The badge of authority, authority itself, was unquestioned. Nobody questioned authority. It probably worked because it suited the social culture of the Indian people, Shuswaps particularly — they were the only ones I really knew well. They were subjected to a chief by a culture that was very demanding. And the authority was very very strict and it was accepted. It was never questioned anymore than it was in any other society. But, by 1942, that was not accepted anymore at all.

The authority on the reserves had changed very very rapidly. The courts had long since been forced out of existence. I shouldn't say the Indians disapproved; they just ignored. These fines and things, they had vanished. It could have been just a year or so, but I know they were gone when I got there. The interpreter was tolerated and you didn't say anything as he was one of the old leaders there. When we went to Alkali Lake reserve and everybody was

76

out on the front lawn on a warm Sunday morning playing gambling games with cards on a blanket and Father Thomas told them to come to Mass, nobody came to Mass because he said so. Those people remained gambling throughout the service. On none of the reserves was there the snap up and click your heels kind of discipline that the Durieu System was intended to inculcate.

I think the lack of communications with the Indians had been a problem for some time by the time I got there and I believe it had weakened an awful lot the relationship between the priest and the Indians. So I felt from the beginning that there was one way of approaching the Indians, that was to speak with them, reason with them. Anything else — Durieu notwithstanding — I could not accept.

MISSIONARY NURSE IN CHILCOTIN COUNTRY

SISTER TERESA BERNARD: I was born in St. Jules de Maria, in the county of Bonaventure, Gaspé Bay in 1914. And we were a family of 11. I went to the country school, which was an English and French school, all the grades from one to six. That was the highest grade we could go. So I stayed in grade six from 12 to 16, to have a teacher certificate I had to wait till I be 16. At 16, I went to Carleton — they had a normal school — where I was there for one year, and after I took the government test for elementary school diploma.

I'd always had the idea of being a Sister. I didn't work for it you know. I went out and I had a boyfriend and all this, but it always bothered me a little bit. So I had in my mind I was just going to try — and come back! So I packed my things and I said, "Now you don't touch my things because I'll be back." I entered the Sisters of Christ the King because my older sister had already entered. So I'd no preference but the fact that she was there. I said, "It doesn't matter where." I was just willing to try. It still bothered me a lot when I was a novice. I was very independent and I didn't care because I still had home in my mind. When I made my first profession all these bad ideas and everything went away.

They just asked me, "Would you like to make a nursing course?" In those days we always say yes. So I went to Montreal and I trained at Hôtel Dieu. I enjoyed my course. The order was just started in 1928, and in maybe '36 they send two or three Sisters to Japan. They were the first ones. They were teaching and the war broke out and we had no communication. My own sister she left for Japan. We had four Sisters teaching at Nelson, the concentration camp for Japanese. They closed that in '44, so they sent back all those Japanese east. In those days Mother Foundress could not send any in mission fields in Japan. You couldn't go anywhere. During that time the Indian missions started. So two Sisters from Nelson and I and another Sister from Montreal, we all met here in Vancouver. Bishop Duke wanted some Sisters for Anaham. But I had you know the false impression that everybody had, the Indians are people that you should not mix with; Indians are people that you should not trust too much — although my own town was near a reserve and my father was very friendly with them.

So we got to Anaham and there was not an Indian on the reserve. They were nomad. They would all disappear in those days. There was not a soul on the reserve. There was just a little house full of flies. There was a tiny little house belonging to the Oblate father and the Indians had built another little log house on the side. This house was only three rooms. In front there was like a parlour and two little rooms in the back. It was too small. And the flies! You were opening your mouth and the flies would get in before you put in the meat.

And we went in the church and we seen . . . oh we were not used to that you know. The bishop had been there in June and see, his throne was still there, and they had put decoration at Christmas all over the church. It was all hanging down all over. And after, they never made the cleaning, and there was cobwebs everywhere. We didn't understand the Indians' custom because we shouldn't have touch that. It's true. We went in the church and we clean up. We took everything down, which we shouldn't have done. Now I see all the mistakes we made. Reminds me of that Irish song "The English came to show us their ways." Well, it's the same. We went there with the idea of show them how to live and show our ways.

We arrived there about August 27 — the end of August — school was supposed to start the beginning of September. Sister Marie des Anges and Sister Stanislaus, the two of them were teachers. There was nobody there. Nothing was built, and September was going on. The week after, they all came down from the meadow, from nowhere. They were all camping, there was hardly any houses. They all had tent and they tented around us. It was just like a village of little tents.

And after, they started. And the way they work you know they work five, six would work together and the others were all sitting there and talking together. They will work for maybe an hour or so and they will exchange. But they just had $500 for that, that was just the material. They were not getting very much in those days from the government. So they put the walls and they put the windows and they put the roof, but the inside it wasn't finished. So when the $500 was over, they all went home. You know it's cold, it's 40 below out there. So we said, "We can't stay like this." There was a saw, there was some paper so we started to put paper on some walls — building paper — when we were all finished that, they got some kind of beaver board or something like this and Father Bede from Williams Lake he came up and he covered up all the inside of that building.

After we had these quarters we slept there, so the two little rooms we didn't need it, so we said we will make a chapel with one. We had no tabernacle or no altar so I said, "I'll have to make one." First time it was all crooked you know but after I could saw very well. So that was my first masterpiece!

There was two classrooms, those who had already been to school — they were about 12 I think — and in the other one there were maybe 40 — they had never been to school. They were all different ages. So this was okay and we went on, but these people were not used to stay on the reserve. They had meadows far away, and they had cattle and they used to hunt. When they used to go they used to bring the whole family. So they hadn't thought about this. They didn't know when they had asked for a school that they would have to stay down and look after the children, or keep the children home, down for school. But Christmastime came, and the snow, but they said they had to go and feed their cattle. So after Christmas we had maybe six in the school.

After a while, little by little, they stayed longer on the reserve, and they are just a few families that kept their children from an education. Some had had an education before, but some of those didn't. They couldn't see the

Opposite: Sister Teresa Bernard (or Mother St. Paul as she was known then) taking a perilous route across the Chilcotin River when the spring thaw destroyed the bridge. She was taking a baby home to Stoney Reserve, and going to visit a mother and her new-born baby (Sister Teresa Bernard).

reason to have an education. Shoot a moose, shoot a squirrel, you don't need to know to read and write. They didn't believe in it. Said it was just wasted time for them.

Bishop Duke always had in his mind to start an Indian community and we got a little girl — Sister James from Nanaimo I think, she was only a postulant. He wanted to have a native community so in '45 the bishop ask Father Sutherland to go in all the residential schools — and there were lots in those days — and make propaganda. So in that year a whole bunch of girls came — five or six — but they didn't stay very long. Some came from Mission, one from Pavillion, another was from North Van. Andy Paull, his girl, well his daughter didn't stay very long. Of that group two stayed, one named Sacred Heart and the other was named Incarnation. They took the habit.

They stayed maybe a year, two years; one after the other they left. We had another one from Smithers. That one made profession. Bishop Duke send her on a propaganda tour to pick up some other girls and she went to some place — in Le Pas, Manitoba they have a Métis congregation — so she, instead of finding him some recruits, she joined their community. Bishop Duke was very very happy with all these recruits and he thought that they would grow up in the community in no time. So he decided to build the convent.

I don't think they realized too much what they were to relinquish. They had no idea what was religious life. We would go and make our prayers and they would be by themselves and they will run after the boys on the reserve. The Chilcotin boys would call them Shuswaps if they want to insult them. But they didn't realize too much what was religious life.

At the beginning it was funny. We started a nursing home — that old building down there — at the beginning I didn't have any experience. You know you train in a hospital. In a hospital you have young doctors, you're not supposed to give any medication without being prescribed, you are not supposed to do anything without it's ordered, and you are sent way back in the field, all by yourself, there's nobody to help you. At the beginning I find it so hard.

A nursing Sister of Christ the King visits Redstone Indians to check on their health. (Sister Teresa Bernard).

In 1947 the first group of Indian girls to enter the Anaham novitiate enjoy the winter weather with Sister Lise Bernard. (Sister Teresa Bernard).

And besides that I was French. I had studied in French and to translate all this in English I didn't know the medical words. You train and you learn all the technique and the words that go with it. And the Indians in those days they didn't know very many English. They knew maybe four, five words. So I was trying to get the message to them. It was *so hard* and I didn't know them. They'd bring the children and after they'd stay around the house to see if the child was crying. They don't trust us. But it didn't take very long. It was the other way round. They would bring them all. They would want to go to stampede, and *all* their baby were sick you know.

Sister Bernard — another Sister the same name as I — she was driving for me. Everytime we would go for the sick — they would call me in — and I would visit them in those reserves, Redstone, Stoney, oh any place in the Chilcotin. There's not a place I didn't go. Riske Creek, Nemiah Valley, impractical places they were — Eagle Lake. And never anything happened. I have in my mind you know that Obedience send me there and He wants me to do it and I'm going to do it and this is all. Oh I went some terrible places.

Just got lost once. I was taking a baby home and an Indian put a mark at the road where to turn off. When finally I find a guide he said, "Now can you take me to my camp?" It was getting quite dark. I said, "Well, yes, I suppose." Put the baby on a horse and by the time he gets home with the baby he's going to be sick again! And coming back there was no road, and I got stuck one place and I could hardly see the road. I was alone you know. Usually I wait for my companion — another Sister used to come with me — but she wasn't ready. I was impatient in those days, I didn't wait.

They were still believing quite a bit in the medicine man. And they would — not doing it openly — but they would go and get the medicine man and sometimes I know I had to wait at the door and they will tell me, "Oh well they're doing something inside. You can go after." And after they will say, "You can go" but they had used a medicine man first, and after, me; and after they would probably call the priest. They wouldn't take any chance. No, they would use every possible means.

I admire the simplicity in their religion. Very simple, very strong. Like holy water. Well, I like holy water but I cannot have that faith that they have in holy water. And I'm sure holy water did miracle for them, because they never went to the meadows without having gone to the priest and have holy water blessed. And I'm sure even holy water made miracles for them, got them better in the meadows when they were all by themselves. They would have that faith.

A NEW MISSIONARY'S ROLE

FATHER JOHN HENNESSY: I was born in Vancouver in 1910. One of the things I can remember was that my father was really active in the church and particularly in chauffering missionaries around. In those days there were many priests coming out on their way to the Orient and my father would be always taking them around town so priests were quite common in our house. When I was about 14 we moved into St. Pat's parish where Father Forgé was; he was quite famous when it comes to vocations. He sent 10 of us to the Oblate Junior Seminary, St. John's College. It just seemed to be that that was what I wanted to do.

Sister Teresa Bernard and Sister Lucianna check the health of some Chilcotin Indians, 1947. (Sister Teresa Bernard).

Indian graveyard at the Ulkatcho settlement. (BCPM, Ethnology Division, photo no. PN 3299).

I was ordained in '34. In those days you wrote to the Superior General telling him what you would like to do as an Oblate. And I wanted to go out into the country. I'd been raised in the city but I had a great desire to go out into the country. And I got my request, I was sent to Williams Lake to work with Father Thomas.

In the fall I began looking after what we call the north side of the Fraser; that was Marguarite and Quesnel and Nasko, Kluskus, Ulkatcho, Redstone, Anaham, Stoney and Riske Creek. I don't think I changed things that greatly. I didn't initiate any new programs amongst the people except coming more frequently. I think I mixed with them a little more, visited them in their homes.

The one thing I did do was in 1941, I started a seasonal school at Redstone. In Redstone — which was way off the beaten track — there was no education. They wanted a school but they didn't want to send their kids to what they called the Mission School. There seemed to be no possibility of getting a complete day care because they were still nomadic. They would be leaving with their families in the spring to go fishing, hunting and trapping. Then in summer and fall they were working on their own lands haying or with white people. So from the end of October to the first of March seemed to be an ideal time.

The Indian department volunteered to provide the books and to pay me. I was paid $125 a month as a teacher, but I had no qualifications. None. I simply tried to teach them how to read and write. They used the church on what was known as Redstone Meadows, a church that was on the property in which the chief was living. A number of people had built their own little cabins there just for "priest time" as they called it. So in November the parents were going back to the meadows to feed their cattle would simply leave the children there with me. The older children looked after the younger children. And I was sort of a watchman.

They enjoyed the school. The kids they came willingly. We started about nine-thirty and we ended about two-thirty and there was no particular schedule. They learned to read and write. That's what they wanted. I wasn't equipped to give them a full education and they weren't ready to accept it either. The scheme proved itself when at the end of six years, one of those lads was arrested for forging a cheque. He'd reached the stage where he could now write other peoples' names besides his own!

I got to know them better than I had before. The old chief, Charlie Boy, would tell me some of their legends and traditions. I began to realize that they had a culture which was particularly theirs. I don't think I realized, what I now know, that they were a people unto themselves. Because they were still bush

Anaham Indian Reserve and Chilcotin women. Photograph by W. W. Stevens, 1923.
(BCPM, Ethnology Division, photo no. PN 3338).

Chilcotin children from Anaham Reserve in their First Communion finery.
(BCPM, Ethnology Division, photo no. PN 14004).

people in a sense. They accepted me even though I was part of the establishment. That was to come out later on; they coupled the Church with the establishment and therefore turned off both. But at that time, no. But there was less and less — how shall I put it? — less and less paternal relationships between the priest and the people. They didn't look upon the priest with the same, I guess you might say reverence and respect that their parents did.

I started going much more frequently; once I got a car in 1940 I would go quite regularly. Now regularly didn't mean every week. Father Thomas believed that it was wrong to go every Sunday. That they weren't ready for that. It was better for them to have it occasionally as they did, maybe four times a year in the Chilcotin. Twice a year up at Nasko, once a year in Kluskus and Ulkatcho.

Bishop Johnson wanted a priest on every reserve. Many of the missionaries I spoke to were in two minds about that; first of all whether this was good, whether this fitted into the Indian rhythm, that their rhythm didn't go for something that was set every week. Others thought too that they were imposing an obligation upon Indians that they were never going to keep — to go to church every Sunday. At Chilcotin they couldn't because there were months when they weren't home. They would leave Anaham in the winter once the snow fell and go up in the meadows 30 or 40 miles where their cattle were. Then they came back when the priest would come, maybe after three or four months. And that seemed to be a good pattern.

I went more frequently and I think at that time they were ready for that. So instead of going four times a year I would go maybe eight times. And the same in the Ulkatcho. I use to go into Anahim Lake and then ride — go by mostly pack horse — to Ulkatcho reserve. Maybe two or three times a year we'd get in there.

Whether we achieved any greater results I don't know. But at least they knew that we were concerned and doing what we could to help them. But I think what I suffered from, in all honesty, was that complete lack of training. I came out of the seminary with no training whatsoever in regard to the work I was to do. I really wasn't sure what I should do. Today a missionary can go away and spend three or four months studying the work pattern of other missionaries in other countries, or with Indians say in Eastern Canada. We had nothing like that. We had a complete ignorance of the Indian, not only his language but his whole background. There was little written about the Indian in those days. All we had was Father Morice's study of the Déné people. With no sociological background, I think we were fortunate that we achieved what we did. But maybe we did more harm than good. Maybe our approach was wrong from the beginning.

Many feel it would have been far better for the Indian people if they'd had the day school instead of the residential school. But the missionaries felt they had to get the children there to catechize them, because the parents were on the move, they were nomadic, which was true. I don't think that's completely true that the children were removed to keep them from the influences of the Indian family. But I know that's certainly partly true. And very often the children were forcibly removed whether the parents liked it or not. Again you have this same mentality that these are not only a minority group but an inferior group. So you treat them with force.

I remember Bishop O'Conner being highly incensed when the children were transferred from the Mission and sent to the public school in Williams Lake. Not that he was opposed to education or intermingling but he said their parents were never consulted by the Department. Suddenly the ruling came. Nobody went to the parents and said, "What do you think of this?" There was no communication. They were always wards of the government. This was unfortunate, and I think this has hurt them more than anything else. Because they suffered from that paternalism of the government and the church.

The only time they asked me to help [in a material sense] was during the war when, in the Chilcotin they would be getting letters to come down and to be physically examined when conscription came in. I felt for most of them it was useless. They were Indians in the bush, they would — as a whole — never fit into army life. So I just said to them, forget it. They could hardly talk English a lot of them. They were flat-footed because they wore moccasins. I couldn't see how they'd ever pass inspection. For them to go all the way to Vancouver — which they had to — would have entailed not only great cost but also a great sacrifice. So I didn't encourage them to go down; let's put it that way. Whatever it was that came, the letter, they just put it in the furnace and burnt it. And this got back to the RCMP and I was put on the suspect list. I was encouraging the Indians not to participate in the war effort. I guess under the *War Measures Act* I was suspect. In fact at one time they were threatening to take some civil action.

Alice Johnny and Sister Bernadette attend to a small patient at the Anaham Reserve, circa 1949-55. (BCPM, Ethnology Division, photo no. PN 13330).

I felt satisfied with the work I had done. I wasn't too sure though what I had accomplished. Of course hindsight is so much easier than foresight. It was really a cultic service I was rendering. It was Mass and the sacraments. Of course there was nothing else that you could offer them in those days. This was what Catholics . . . how they lived, how they practised. So in a sense I say I thought I did my duty and had done it as well as I could. I was sorry to leave because I was enjoying the work and the people. I was looking forward to being with them longer.

CONCLUSION

The efforts of the early missionaries to Christianize the Indian peoples of British Columbia met with qualified success. While a large percentage of the Indians found something to attract them in the Christian message, many appear to have resisted missionary attempts to completely substitute European religion for their Indian culture. The continued presence of the medicine men and the resurgence of Indian cultural activities in recent years are witness to this resistance. The relationship between the Churches and the Indians however remains. Missionaries still work throughout the province, continuing the historical process begun in 1858. But there are significant differences. The attitudes of the missionaries have changed. As one put it, "I go to visit people, not push religion on them"; another points out that although in the past missionaries used to be "tin gods on pedestals," that has now changed.* The Churches offer highly visible practical help. In July 1981 the Anglican Church accused the federal government of "not bargaining in good faith with the native Indians" and supported Nishga land claims. There is also a new understanding and awareness of Indian culture and values. In July 1979, for example, an Oblate, Terry McNamara — or Xwiselaneexw as the Indians named him — was ordained a priest in the Quamichan longhouse in Duncan. The ceremony was part Indian longhouse ritual and part Roman Catholic ritual.

It is easy to condemn the ethnocentricity of the early missionaries which was responsible to a large extent for the decline of Indian languages and culture. Even today's missionaries have sometimes felt responsible for what was done in the past. But recent writings reveal that the Indian peoples were capable of sound judgment and discernment with regard to the offerings of white civilization and were not merely helpless victims falling before a conquering society. Perhaps the positive response of Indian peoples of the past — who must be credited with having the perception to recognize both good and bad in their missionaries — bears witness to their judgment of the Christian message.

One missionary, Salvation Army Captain Ron Trickett, clearly expressed Indian discernment when making a statement on his work on the Nass River:

> Now the rewards of this work are very great. The rewards I feel far surpass the disappointments that do come. The friendships that develop are lifelong, lasting and real. Native people have a way of understanding, far greater than we can understand, whether we really are for them, whether we really like them, whether we're with them and working along with them, or whether we're just preaching at them or to them. They can understand in a very deep way, whether we are people who are really committed to helping them or whether we are only out for our own interests. Amongst the native people, the culture may be a little different, the traditions are definitely different in many ways, and the habits are a little different sometime, but the Creator is the same.

---

* Unidentified newspaper clipping in the possession of the author.

BIOGRAPHICAL SUMMARIES

CHIEF ROY AZAK: A prominent member of the Wolf Clan of Canyon City (Git-winksihlk), small village on the Nass River and the only entirely Salvation Army village established on or near the coast.
(Interviewed by Norman Newton, June 1962. PABC No. 2148)

SISTER TERESA BERNARD (born 1914): A French-Canadian from the Gaspé Peninsula, Sister Teresa (Mother St. Paul) is a missionary nursing nun. She came to British Columbia in 1944, and spent many years providing medical services for the Indian peoples.
(Interviewed by Margaret Whitehead, January 9, 1981. PABC No. 3867)

MARGARET BOOTH (born 1919): Mrs. Booth (née Sansum) was born in New Westminster, the first child born to Methodist missionary Reverend Victor Harold Sansum and his wife Patricia. Margaret spent much of her childhood living on the Indian reserves at Kispiox and Port Simpson.
(Interviewed by Margaret Whitehead, December 6, 1980. PABC No. 3866)

WILLIAM (BILL) CHRISTIE (born 1898): Born in Drumlichie, Kincardinshire, Scotland, Bill Christie came to Canada in 1919. After a decade on the prairies, he brought his wife and family to British Columbia where, during the Depression, he became Indian Agent, first at Bella Coola, and later, in 1945, at Williams Lake.
(Interviewed by Margaret Whitehead, June 1, 1979. PABC No. 3534)

MARY ENGLUND (born 1904): Mrs. Englund was born in Lillooet. Her early years were spent at Bralorne and D'Arcy Indian reserve but, at the age of eight, she was taken to the Mission Indian Residential School where she remained until she was 16.
(Interviewed by Margaret Whitehead, July 31, 1980. PABC No. 3868)

FATHER JOHN HENNESSY (born 1910): The son of a professional lacrosse player, Father Hennessy grew up in Vancouver. At 14, he entered St. John's College, Edmonton, the Oblate Junior Seminary. Later he attended both Lebrett Scholasticate and the Oblate Seminary in Ottawa. Father Hennessy has worked both as Indian missionary and Indian school principal.
(Interviewed by Margaret Whitehead, June 19, 1980. PABC No. 3716)

CHIEF CLARENCE JOE (born 1908): He was of the hereditary line of the Sechelt chiefs. He was appointed by Ottawa to be acting chief until Ottawa approved an elective government.
(Interviewed by Imbert Orchard, 1965. PABC Nos. 960 and 2478)

AGNES (KATHY) JOHNSON: Mrs. Johnson (née Tomlinson) is the daughter of Richard Tomlinson who was the second son born to Robert and Alice Tomlinson.
(Interviewed by Imbert Orchard, July 12, 1961. PABC No. 2460)

CELESTINE JOHNSON (born 1899): Mrs. Johnson lives at Alkali Lake reserve in the Cariboo. At the age of six, she was taken to the Cariboo Indian Residential School, known locally as the Mission.
(Interviewed by Margaret Whitehead, June 7, 1979. PABC No. 3532)

DAVID JOHNSON (born 1895): Like his wife Celestine, David Johnson attended the Mission. In the 1940s, he was elected chief of Alkali Lake.
(Interviewed by Margaret Whitehead, June 7, 1979. PABC No. 3532)

ANNIE MOBERLY (born 1879): A daughter of Robert and Alice Tomlinson, Mrs. Moberly was born at Ankatlas, a Christian Indian community established by her father the year of her birth.
(Interviewed by Imbert Orchard, July 12, 1961. PABC No. 1198)

FATHER ALEX MORRIS (born 1911): A native of the Gaspé region of Quebec, Father Morris was educated for the priesthood in Ottawa. In 1942, he was sent "temporarily" to British Columbia but he remained in the province acting as both Indian missionary and Indian school principal.
(Interviewed by Margaret Whitehead, July 30, 1980. PABC No. 3869)

SISTER PATRICIA (born 1893): Sister Patricia (born Josephine Tuite) came to Canada from Ireland in 1911. She joined the Sisters of the Child Jesus and has worked at several missionary schools throughout the province.
(Interviewed by Margaret Whitehead, July 8, 1980. PABC No. 3533)

LILLY SQUINAHAN: Mrs. Squinahan lives at Alkali Lake reserve. As a child, she attended the Mission school.
(Interviewed by Margaret Whitehead, June 7, 1979. PABC No. 3530)

ROBERT TOMLINSON, JR. (born 1870): The oldest son of Robert and Alice Tomlinson, Robert Jr. remained with his father, working in the Christian Indian villages of New Metlakatla (Alaska) and Minskinisht. After his father's death, he was the Methodist missionary at Kispiox.
(Recorded by Mrs. Robert Tomlinson Jr. [his second wife] in 1955; and interviewed by Mrs. Walter T. Stewert, 1955. PABC No. 1238)

MRS. ROBERT TOMLINSON, JR. (born 1897): Born in Winnipeg, Manitoba, Mrs. Tomlinson, Jr. was sent to Glen Vowell, British Columbia, as a Salvation Army missionary. There she met her future husband, who was working at Kispiox, three miles from Glen Vowell.
(Interviewed by Imbert Orchard, July 12, 1961. PABC No. 1227)

RONALD TRICKETT: Officer-in-charge of the Salvation Army church at Canyon City on the Nass River.
(Interviewed by Norman Newton, June 1962. PABC No. 2148)

A NOTE ON SOURCES

The material used for this edition of *Sound Heritage Series* is a combination of oral and written information. Apart from the books cited in the introduction, all other material is from primary sources.

The bulk of the material consists of interviews which were recorded on tape. These tapes are available for study purposes at the Sound and Moving Image Division of the Provincial Archives of British Columbia.

In order to verify an incident, to expand a topic, or simply to give added interest, information from original documents has been inserted. Some have been cited in footnotes; those not already cited can be found in the Oblate Archives in Vancouver, and in the Archives Deschâtalets, Ottawa.

VISUAL CREDITS

PUBLIC SOURCES

British Columbia Provincial Museum, Ethnology Division: front cover, ii, 13, 14, 18, 33, 58, 83, 84, 85, 87, inside back cover.

Provincial Archives of British Columbia, Historic Photographs: 3, 6, 8.

Provincial Archives of British Columbia, Manuscripts: 9.

Provincial Archives of British Columbia, Paintings, Drawings and Prints: 10, 15.

Archives Deschâtalets, Ottawa: 26, 30, 32, 38.

Public Archives of Canada, National Photography Collection: 43.

PRIVATE SOURCES

Sister Teresa Bernard: inside front cover, 68, 76, 79, 80, 81, 82.

John Veillette: 20, 21, 24.

Margaret Whitehead: 35, 40.

John Brioux, OMI: 45, 48, 52.

Celestine Johnson: 46.

Sister Patricia: 54.

Alex Morris: 56.

Mary Englund: 62, 66.

Mrs. Margaret Booth: 71, 72, 73, back cover.

MAPS

Mary-Lynn Ogilvie: iv.

Sono Nis Press, Victoria: 28.

DESIGN

David Mattison and Margaret Whitehead.

SOUND HERITAGE SERIES

Provincial Archives of British Columbia
Victoria, B.C., Canada V8V 1X4
(Price subject to change without notice)

SOUND HERITAGE SERIES, upcoming issues.......................................$10 for four numbers
(by prepaid subscription)

JOURNALISM IN BRITISH COLUMBIA BETWEEN THE WARS (working title)
by Peter Stursberg.
Cassette Sound Program, $2.50.

FLOODLAND AND FOREST (working title)
Life in the Fraser Valley (double issue—counts as two).
by Imbert Orchard.
Cassette Sound Program, $2.50.

SCANDINAVIAN SETTLEMENTS ON THE COAST (working title)
by Gordon Fish.
Cassette Sound Program, $2.50.

EARLY RADIO IN BRITISH COLUMBIA (working title)
by Dennis Duffy.
Cassette Sound Program, $2.50.

SOUND HERITAGE SERIES BACKLIST

(Prices subject to change without notice)

No. 34 NOW YOU ARE MY BROTHER: MISSIONARIES IN BRITISH COLUMBIA $3.00
by Magaret Whitehead, 92 pp.

No. 33 SETTLING CLAYOQUOT.. $3.00
Vancouver Island's West Coast, 76 pp.
Cassette Sound Program, *Castle Island and Other Stories of Clayoquot Sound*, $2.50.

No. 32 WHERE THE LARDEAU RIVER FLOWS $3.00
Recollections of the Kootenay Region, 84 pp.
Cassette Sound Program, *Legends of the Lardeau: The Stories of Red McLeod and Andy Daney*, $2.50.

No. 31 RAILROADERS.. $3.00
Recollections of the Steam Era on British Columbia's Railroads.
Cassette Sound Program, *Avalanche Mountain*, $2.50.

No. 30 MARTIN — THE STORY OF A YOUNG FUR TRADER.................... $3.00
The northern reminiscences of Martin Starret, 76 pp.
Cassette Sound Programs, *Travellers of the North* and *The Childhood of Martin Starret*,
$2.50 each.

No. 29 SEASON'S GREETINGS FROM BRITISH COLUMBIA'S PAST.......... $3.00
Christmas as celebrated by British Columbia residents, 1880–1930, 74 pp.
Cassette Sound Program, *Sounds of Christmas Past*, $2.50.

No. 28 THE MAGNIFICENT DISTANCES $3.00
Early Aviation in British Columbia, 1910–1940, 78 pp.
Cassette Sound Program, *From Jericho Beach to Swanson Bay*, $2.50.

Opposite: Indians building St. Paul's Church at Kitwanga, circa 1890s.
(BCPM, Ethnology Division, photo no. PN 7798).

SOUND HERITAGE SERIES BACKLIST

No. 34 ($3)

No. 33 ($3)

No. 32 ($3)

No. 31 ($3)

No. 30 ($3)

No. 29 ($3)

No. 28 ($3)

No. 27 ($3)

No. 26 ($3)

Order Sound Heritage Series back copies

I would like to order the following *Sound Heritage Series* back issues:

☐ 14 ($3) ☐ 16 ($3) ☐ 18 ($3) ☐ 19 ($3) ☐ 20 ($3) ☐ 21 ($3)
☐ 22 ($3) ☐ 23 ($3) ☐ 24/25 ($6) ☐ 26 ($3) ☐ 27 ($3) ☐ 28 ($3)
☐ 29 ($3) ☐ 30 ($3) ☐ 31 ($3) ☐ 32 ($3) ☐ 33 ($3) ☐ 34 ($3)

Please enclose payment ☐ (Make cheques payable to Minister of Finance, Province of British Columbia.)

Name...

Address ....

....

.... Postal Code.................

(Signed)...

Subscribe to the Sound Heritage Series

I would like............ year(s) subscription to the *Sound Heritage Series* at $10 per year (4 issues).

Payment enclosed ☐
(Make cheques payable to the Minister of Finance, Province of British Columbia.)

OFFICE USE ONLY		
I/D Alpha................................		
☐ A	☐ C	☐ D
List Type	Dist.	

Renewal ☐   Gift subscription ☐

Name..

Address ....

....

.... Postal Code.................

Signed...

No. 24/25 ($6)

No. 23 ($3)

No. 22 ($3)

No. 21 ($3)

No. 20 ($3)

No. 19 ($3)

No. 18 ($3)

No. 16 ($3)

No. 14 ($3)

**Province of
British Columbia**

Ministry of Provincial Secretary
and Government Services
PROVINCIAL ARCHIVES

SOUND HERITAGE SERIES
Sound and Moving Image Division
Provincial Archives of British Columbia
Parliament Buildings
Victoria, B.C.
Canada V8V 1X4

**Province of
British Columbia**

Ministry of Provincial Secretary
and Government Services
PROVINCIAL ARCHIVES

SOUND HERITAGE SERIES
Sound and Moving Image Division
Provincial Archives of British Columbia
Parliament Buildings
Victoria, B.C.
Canada V8V 1X4